DEDALO AGENCY

ICELAND
Travel guide

**HOW TO PLAN
A TRIP TO ICELAND
WITH BEST TIPS
FOR FIRST-TIMERS**

Edited by: Domenico Russo and Francesco Umbria
Design e layout: Giorgia Ragona
Book series: Journey Joy

© 2023 DEDALO SRLS
Iceland Travel guide
How to Plan a Trip to Iceland
with Best Tips for First-Timers

www.agenziadedalo.it

ICELAND
Travel guide

Foreword

In the following pages of the book, you will find essential advice on what to see and do in Iceland, and there will be specific insights to enjoy your trip to the fullest (even without spending exorbitant amounts).

The travel guide series of the Journey Joy collection was designed to be lean and straight to the point. The idea of keeping the guides short required significant work in synthesis, in order to guide the reader towards the essential destinations and activities within each country or city.

If you like the book, leaving a positive review can help us spread our work. We realize that leaving a review can be a tedious activity, so we want to give you a gift. Send an email to **bonus@dedaloagency.net**, attach the screenshot of your review, and you will get completely **FREE**, in your mailbox, **THE UNRELEASED EBOOK**: "The Art of Traveling: Essential Tips for Unforgettable Journeys".

Remember to check the Spam folder, as the email might end up there!

We thank you in advance and wish you to always travel and enjoy every adventure!

Index

FOREWORD	4
INTRODUCTION	11
CHAPTER 1: REYKJAVIK	19
Hallgrímskirkja	20
Harpa Concert Hall	20
Old Harbour	21
Laugavegur Shopping Street	22
Reykjavik Art Museum	23
National Museum of Iceland	24
The Sun Voyager	24
Whale Watching from Reykjavik	25
Reykjavik by Night	26
Day Trip to Videy Island	26
Reykjavik Cuisine	27
Final Thoughts	28
CHAPTER 2: GOLDEN CIRCLE	33
Thingvellir National Park	34
Geysir Geothermal Area	34
Gullfoss Waterfall	35
Kerid Crater Lake	36
Faxi Waterfall	36
Secret Lagoon in Flúðir	37
Efstidalur II (Farm and Restaurant)	37
Icelandic Horses	38
Laugarvatn Fontana	39
Flora and Fauna	39
Historical Significance	40
Exploring the Golden Circle by Night	41
Final Thoughts	41

Chapter 3: South Coast — 47

- Seljalandsfoss Waterfall — 48
- Skógafoss Waterfall — 48
- Reynisfjara Black Sand Beach — 49
- Vik Village — 50
- Dyrhólaey Peninsula — 50
- Solheimajokull Glacier — 51
- Jokulsarlon Glacier Lagoon — 51
- Diamond Beach — 52
- South Coast by Night — 53
- Day Trip to Vestmannaeyjar — 53
- South Coast Cuisine — 54
- Final Thoughts — 54

Chapter 4: Westfjords — 59

- Dynjandi Waterfall — 60
- Latrabjarg Cliffs — 60
- Raudasandur Beach — 61
- Isafjordur Town — 62
- Hornstrandir Nature Reserve — 62
- Hot Springs of Westfjords — 63
- Westfjords by Night — 64
- Road Trip Around Westfjords — 64
- Boat Tours from Isafjordur — 65
- Wildlife Spotting in Westfjords — 65
- Westfjords Cuisine — 66
- Final Thoughts — 66

Chapter 5: Eastfjords — 73

- Seydisfjordur — 74
- Borgarfjordur Eystri — 75
- Papey Island — 76
- Eastfjords Wildlife — 76
- Hallormsstadur National Forest — 77
- The Hidden Waterfalls of Eastfjords — 77
- Eastfjords' Small Villages Exploration — 78
- Eastfjords by Night — 79
- Day Trip to Storurd — 79
- Fjords Hiking — 80

Eastfjords Cuisine	81
Final Thoughts	81

Chapter 6: North Iceland — 87

Akureyri	88
Lake Myvatn	88
Husavik Whale Watching	89
Dettifoss Waterfall	90
Godafoss Waterfall	90
The Arctic Henge	91
Lofthellir Ice Cave	91
Tröllaskagi Peninsula	92
Ásbyrgi Canyon	93
The Beer Spa	93
North Iceland by Night	94
Day Trip to Grímsey Island	94
North Iceland Cuisine	95
Final Thoughts	96

Chapter 7: Snaefellsnes Peninsula — 101

Snaefellsjokull National Park	102
Kirkjufell Mountain	103
Budir Black Church	103
Fishing Villages of Snaefellsnes	104
Djupalonssandur Beach	105
Gerðuberg Basalt Cliffs	105
Vatnshellir Cave	106
Snaefellsnes Peninsula by Night	107
Day Trip to Stykkisholmur	107
Snaefellsnes Road Trip	108
Snaefellsnes Cuisine	108
Final Thoughts	109

Chapter 8: Highlands — 115

Landmannalaugar	116
Thorsmork	117
Askja	117
Rhyolite Mountains	118
Vatnajökull Glacier	119
Kerlingarfjoll Mountains	120

INDEX — 7

Hiking in the Highlands	120
Highlands by Night	121
Day Trip to Hveravellir	122
Laugavegur Trail	123
Highlands Cuisine	123
Final Thoughts	124

CHAPTER 9: REYKJANES PENINSULA — 129

Blue Lagoon	130
Gunnuhver Geothermal Area	131
Bridge Between Continents	131
Reykjanes Lighthouse	132
Krysuvik-Seltun	132
Volcanic Fissures	133
Viking World Museum	134
Reykjanes Peninsula by Night	134
Day Trip to Grindavik	135
Exploring Reykjanes by Car	136
Reykjanes Cuisine	137
Final Thoughts	137

CHAPTER 10: ICELANDIC CUISINE — 143

Skyr	144
Lamb	145
Fish and Seafood	145
Rye Bread	146
Hot Dogs	147
Traditional Fermented Shark	147
Icelandic Candy	148
Local Dining Spots	148
Food Festivals	149
Regional Specialties	150
Vegetarian and Vegan Cuisine	150
Final Thoughts	151

CHAPTER 11: HOW TO TRAVEL ICELAND ON A BUDGET — 155

Choosing the Right Time to Visit	156
Accommodation	157
Food and Drinks	157
Transportation	158

Sightseeing and Attractions	159
Shopping	159
Avoiding Tourist Traps	160
Using Local Currency	160
Travel Insurance	161
Bargaining	162
Eco-friendly Practices	162
Final Thoughts	163

Chapter 12: 10 Cultural Experiences You Must Try in Iceland — 167

1. Attending a Local Festival	168
2. Bathing in a Geothermal Pool	168
3. Witnessing the Northern Lights	169
4. Visiting a Traditional Turf House	169
5. Horse Riding	170
6. Whale Watching	171
7. Hiking on a Glacier	171
8. Experiencing Midnight Sun	172
9. Sampling Traditional Icelandic Cuisine	173
10. Experiencing a Traditional Icelandic Sagas Storytelling	173
Final Thoughts	174

Conclusion	177
Final notes	181

INDEX — 9

Introduction

Welcome, dear traveller, to a land of striking contrasts and incredible beauty: Iceland. As you embark on this journey, allow me to introduce you to a place where fire meets ice, where the northern lights dance in the sky, and where the landscapes will leave you breathless. This isn't just a travel guide, it's an invitation to immerse yourself into the authentic Icelandic experience, exploring not just the sights, but the tastes, sounds, and soul of this remarkable land.

Bounded by the fierce North Atlantic Ocean, Iceland sits at the crossroads between continents, a place where the North American and Eurasian tectonic plates pull apart - quite literally. This unique geographical positioning contributes to its striking, ever-changing landscapes that promise a distinct experience. One minute you might be hiking through lush valleys crisscrossed by crystalline rivers, the next you might find yourself in a desolate black sand beach, with towering icebergs floating just offshore.

Every corner of this remarkable island offers something new to be discovered. From the silent tranquillity of the Eastfjords, the rugged beauty of the Snæfellsnes Peninsula, to the endless plains of the Icelandic Highlands. Each place comes with its unique spirit and countless opportunities for adventure. It's no wonder that the island has been a favourite destination for photographers, nature lovers, and wanderers in search of the unusual.

And let's not forget the wildlife. Iceland is a paradise for birdwatchers, with hundreds of species, including the charming puffins, calling this place home. The island's surrounding waters are also teeming with life. A boat trip into the open ocean could bring you face-to-face with majestic whales and playful seals.

At the heart of your journey, you will find the Icelandic people - warm, inviting, and resilient, much like their homeland. Their rich history, old sagas and fascinating Norse mythology will come to life as you visit ancient archaeological sites and museums. The echoes of the Vikings can be heard if you listen closely. In a place where the summer sun barely sets, and the winter darkness is illuminated by the mystical aurora borealis, the rhythm of life is different. By the time you finish your journey, you'll find that you have synced to it - a bit slower, a bit more deliberate, a bit more in harmony with nature.

So, whether you're standing on the edge of a powerful waterfall, hiking on a glacier, soaking in a hot spring, or simply enjoying the stillness of a secluded black sand beach, Iceland encourages you to embrace the moment. It asks you to not just see, but to observe; not just hear, but to listen; not just touch, but to feel. It's an experience that remains with you long after you've left its shores.

This guide aims to be your trusted companion in this journey, not just showing you where to go, but how to truly experience Iceland in all its ethereal beauty and stark contrasts. Because Iceland is not just a destination; it's an experience, an adventure, a story waiting to be told. Now, let's turn the page and begin this extraordinary journey together. Welcome to your Icelandic saga!

Iceland, a small island in the North Atlantic, captivates and inspires like no other. Glittering glaciers slip towards the sea, slicing through a landscape that's as diverse as it is wild. Volcanoes, some silent, some stirring, pepper the horizon while the geothermal heat bubbles up in hot springs and geysers. And let's not forget the mesmerising waterfalls - cascading from high cliffs, they are a humbling sight to behold.

While these natural wonders are undeniably captivating, there is more to this Nordic island than what first meets the eye. Its vibrant cities offer a contrast to the wild outdoors - Reykjavik, the world's northernmost capital, is a lively place, teeming with culture, innovative cuisine, and a nightlife scene that belies the city's small size.

In this guide, we'll traverse through some of the most famous sights, such as the well-trodden path of the Golden Circle, to the untamed beauty of the Westfjords and everything in between. We'll explore the cosmopolitan vibes of Reykjavik, touch the ancient ice at the edges of a glacier, and stand in awe at the base of mighty waterfalls. But we'll also give you a glimpse of some lesser-known gems that will make your journey even more unforgettable.

Food is such a big part of the travel experience and Iceland will not disappoint. In our chapter on Icelandic Cuisine, we'll dive into traditional dishes and culinary delights, from the world-famous skyr to the more acquired taste of fermented shark. You'll also discover local dining spots and food festivals that can provide a unique taste of Icelandic culture.

We understand that travel is not always easy on the wallet, and that's why we've dedicated a whole chapter to how you can make the most of Iceland on a budget. From affordable accommodation to tips on eating out and sightseeing, we'll make sure you have all the information you need to plan a trip that's kind to your budget without missing out on any of the fun.

Iceland isn't just about ticking off the list of must-see places, but about immersing yourself in the experiences and culture of the

INTRODUCTION

country. With this in mind, our chapter on the Top 10 Cultural Experiences will guide you on how to really connect with the heart and soul of Iceland, from bathing in a geothermal pool, experiencing the eerie beauty of the midnight sun, to understanding the country's rich sagas and folklore.

Throughout the book, you'll find personal tips, practical advice, and stories that will help you navigate the country with the ease of someone who has already been there. But remember, while we have provided this guide, the best stories are those that you write yourself. Allow yourself to wander, get lost, and discover. The beauty of travel lies in the unexpected, in the moments that take your breath away, and in the stories you bring back. As you explore Iceland, take your time to breathe in the crisp air, to listen to the roar of a waterfall, to witness the dance of the northern lights, and to savour the taste of adventure. This isn't just a trip; it's a journey into the heart of one of the world's most fascinating countries.

So, grab your warmest clothing, your spirit of adventure, and come with us on this journey across ice and fire.

Welcome to Iceland!

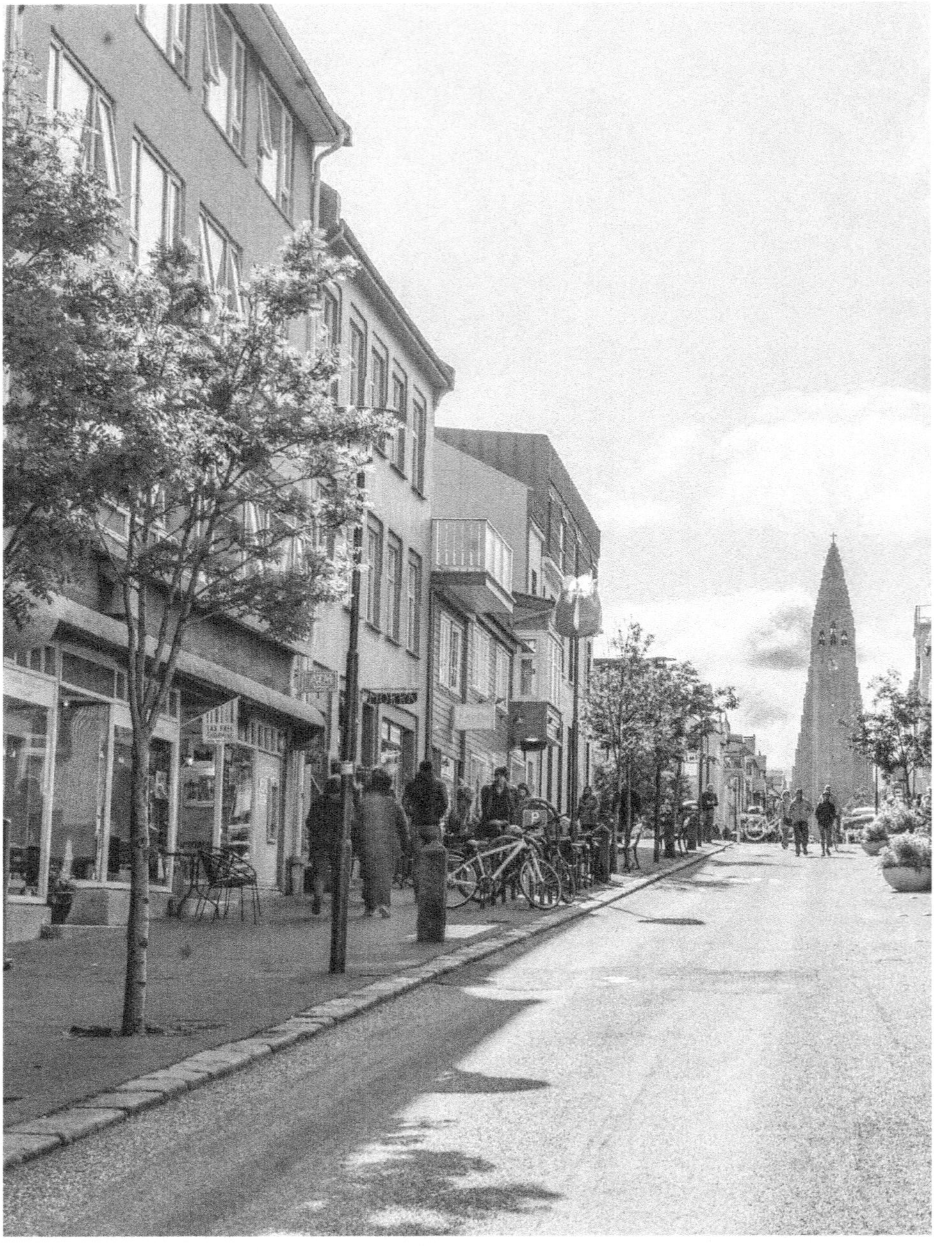

CHAPTER 1: REYKJAVIK 17

CHAPTER 1:
Reykjavik

Unveiling the many wonders of Iceland invariably begins with a dive into its vibrant heart: Reykjavik, the northernmost capital in the world. This colourful city is where modern life mingles harmoniously with the raw, beautiful nature that Iceland is known for. With its vibrant art scene, gastronomical delights, geothermal swimming pools, and a backdrop of snow-capped mountains and the sea, Reykjavik is a city that truly offers something for everyone.

Upon first glance, Reykjavik might seem small, especially when compared to other capital cities, but it's an urban oasis packed with hidden gems. Its compact size is an advantage: you can easily explore the city on foot or bicycle, discovering a myriad of art, history, and culture in its museums, galleries, and architecture.

Reykjavik is also unique in its closeness to nature. In mere minutes, you can go from the city centre to enjoying a quiet hike with panoramic views or to spotting whales in the vast, blue Atlantic. This easy access to nature offers a refreshing take on city life, an experience where urban attractions and outdoor activities coexist.

In the following sections, we'll guide you through the highlights of Reykjavik, from towering architectural feats to intimate local spots. Each location holds a special place in the tapestry of Icelandic life and culture. As we journey together, keep in mind that every location, every bite of Icelandic cuisine, and even the seemingly quiet corners of the city have stories to share.

Hallgrímskirkja

Dominating the skyline of Reykjavik, Hallgrímskirkja is an architectural marvel and one of the most iconic landmarks of the city. Its imposing, 74.5-metre high structure can be seen from nearly every corner of Reykjavik, serving as a unique beacon of the city's spirit.

Designed by the famous Icelandic architect Guðjón Samúelsson, the church's design was inspired by the basalt lava flows found throughout Iceland's extraordinary landscapes. As such, Hallgrímskirkja is not only a place of worship but a testament to the omnipresent influence of nature in Icelandic art and architecture.

Don't miss out on taking the elevator to the observation deck at the top of the tower. From there, you can take in breathtaking panoramic views of Reykjavik's colorful houses, the surrounding mountains, and the sea. It's especially magical during sunrise or sunset, when the light creates a stunning tableau of the city. A small fee applies to access the tower, but the view is well worth the price.

Harpa Concert Hall

The Harpa Concert Hall and Conference Center is another fantastic example of Reykjavik's contemporary architecture. Located by the old harbour, the building is a visual feast with its distinctive coloured glass façade inspired by Iceland's basaltic landscape. It reflects the ever-changing skies and the shimmering waters nearby, creating a living artwork that is continually transforming.

Harpa isn't just an architectural masterpiece; it's the cultural heart of the city. It's home to the Icelandic Symphony Orchestra and the offices of the Icelandic Opera. Attend one of the numerous concerts and cultural events hosted here for an enchanting evening of music in an exceptional setting.

However, even if you do not attend a performance, Harpa is worth visiting for the architecture alone. You can join one of the guided tours to learn more about the building's design and construction or simply enjoy a stroll through its public areas. Don't forget to stop by the higher levels for another fantastic perspective over the old harbour. Finally, before you leave, make sure to explore the Harpa's gift shop where you can find unique Icelandic design items, perfect for a thoughtful souvenir.

Old Harbour

Reykjavik's Old Harbour is a bustling area full of life and character, offering a delightful blend of the old and new. Once a busy fishing port, the harbour has transformed into a vibrant tourist hub while still retaining its authentic charm. The brightly coloured fishing boats and picturesque warehouses make for a beautiful seascape that is uniquely Reykjavik.

Among the old buildings, you will find some of Reykjavik's most popular restaurants and cafes serving fresh seafood and traditional Icelandic dishes. Visit the local fish market to witness the catch of the day or take a leisurely stroll along the waterfront, watching the fishermen at work. The harbour is also the departure point for whale watching tours, puffin excursions, and Northern Lights cruises, providing an easy gateway to explore Iceland's fantastic wildlife.

The Old Harbour area is also home to several interesting museums and galleries, such as the Maritime Museum, which tells the story of Iceland's maritime history and its significance to the country's culture and economy. Close by, you'll also find the Aurora Reykjavik Northern Lights Center, where you can learn all about the fascinating science and folklore behind this natural phenomenon.

Laugavegur Shopping Street

Laugavegur is Reykjavik's main shopping street and the perfect place to immerse yourself in the city's local style and creativity. This lively pedestrian street is lined with boutiques, artisan stores, and vintage shops, offering everything from Icelandic woollen goods and unique jewellery to bespoke furniture and local music records.

As you explore Laugavegur, don't miss the opportunity to discover Icelandic design and fashion. Many local designers have shops here, offering high-quality, unique pieces that embody the Icelandic spirit. Moreover, the street is also home to several stores specializing in traditional hand-knitted "lopapeysa" sweaters, an Icelandic staple that's not just warm but also carries distinctive patterns and design.

Laugavegur is not just about shopping, though. The street is dotted with a variety of eateries and cafes, perfect for grabbing a bite or relaxing with a coffee. After sunset, Laugavegur transforms into a lively nightlife hub, with its many bars and clubs coming to life. Whether you're shopping for souvenirs, enjoying local food, or looking for a fun night out, Laugavegur has something to offer.

Reykjavik Art Museum

The Reykjavik Art Museum is a dynamic and inspiring part of Iceland's cultural scene. As the largest visual art institution in Iceland, the museum houses an extensive collection of works from contemporary and historical artists, both local and international.

The museum is split across three locations: Hafnarhús, Kjarvalsstaðir, and Ásmundarsafn, each offering a different focus. Hafnarhús, located near the Old Harbour, often exhibits progressive contemporary art and houses a significant collection of works by the avant-garde artist Erró. Kjarvalsstaðir, situated in Klambratún park, mainly showcases the works of one of Iceland's most influential artists, Jóhannes S. Kjarval. Ásmundarsafn, a unique building designed by the sculptor Ásmundur Sveinsson, is dedicated to his works and career.

While each site provides a unique artistic perspective, they all offer educational programs, artist talks, and workshops. The museum also operates an excellent café and a well-stocked gift shop, offering reproductions of art works, books, and design products. Remember to check the museum's schedule ahead of your visit as it hosts rotating exhibitions and events, providing fresh and exciting insights into the world of art with each visit.

National Museum of Iceland

The National Museum of Iceland is a treasure trove of historical artifacts and exhibits that chronicle Iceland's rich and unique past. Located in Reykjavik, the museum offers a comprehensive and enlightening view of Iceland's cultural history from settlement to the present day.

The museum's permanent exhibition, "Making of a Nation," displays over 2,000 artifacts and 1,000 photographs. The diverse collection includes Viking-era weapons and tools, medieval manuscripts, ornate church relics, and household objects from different periods, each with a story that contributes to the Icelandic narrative. Interactive displays and multimedia installations make the history come alive, providing a captivating journey through time.

Apart from the permanent exhibition, the museum regularly hosts temporary exhibits on various themes related to Icelandic history and culture. The museum also boasts a child-friendly area, educational activities, and a museum shop offering books, design items, and souvenirs. Visiting the National Museum of Iceland is a must for history buffs and those wanting to gain a deeper understanding of the Icelandic identity.

The Sun Voyager

The Sun Voyager, or 'Sólfar' in Icelandic, is one of Reykjavik's most iconic landmarks. This striking stainless-steel sculpture, designed by Icelandic artist Jón Gunnar Árnason, is located by the sea in the heart of Reykjavik. Resembling a Viking ship, it symbolizes the promise of undiscovered territory, a tribute to the sun, and a dream of hope, progress, and freedom.

The location of the sculpture is significant as it offers a beautiful panoramic view of the bay and Mount Esja across the water. The sculpture's design is such that it appears to be sailing on the sea, offering an ever-changing backdrop with the movement of the sun and the shifting skies.

Visitors often gather at the Sun Voyager for its picture-perfect views, especially during sunrise or sunset when the skies paint a dramatic canvas behind the gleaming sculpture. Remember to take a moment to appreciate not just the art, but the surroundings, the silence, and the vastness of the Icelandic landscape that lies before you.

Whale Watching from Reykjavik

Reykjavik's location by the North Atlantic Ocean makes it an ideal departure point for whale watching tours. A whale watching trip offers the chance to see a variety of marine life in their natural habitat, including minke whales, humpback whales, white-beaked dolphins, and harbour porpoises. On rare occasions, you might even spot an orca or a blue whale.

Several companies operate whale watching tours from the Old Harbour, with experienced guides who provide informative commentary about the marine life and the coastal ecosystem. The boats are equipped with radar and communications equipment to increase the chances of sightings, and some offer hydrophones to listen to the whales' vocalizations underwater.

Remember to dress warmly as it can be quite chilly out at sea, even in summer. Most tours offer warm overalls or blankets. Also, seasickness pills are usually available on board if needed. The experience of seeing these magnificent creatures up close in the wild is an unforgettable experience and a highlight of any trip to Iceland.

Reykjavik by Night

Reykjavik's night scene is as vibrant and diverse as the city itself. When the sun sets, Reykjavik transforms into a bustling hub of entertainment and nightlife, with something to offer everyone. From quiet, cozy bars and high-end restaurants to lively pubs and clubs playing the latest tunes, Reykjavik comes alive when the lights go down.

The city center, especially around Laugavegur and its side streets, is where the nightlife is concentrated. Here, you can find a multitude of bars and clubs offering a range of music genres, local craft beers, and cocktails. Reykjavik's nightlife is known for its "rúntur" or pub crawl, where locals and tourists alike hop from one bar to another, socializing and enjoying the evening.

Remember, nightlife in Reykjavik starts late and goes on until the early hours of the morning, especially on weekends. So, have a leisurely dinner, rest up, and then get ready to experience Reykjavik by night. If you're visiting in winter, you might even get to see the Northern Lights dancing in the sky above you.

Day Trip to Videy Island

Just a short ferry ride from Reykjavik's Old Harbour lies Videy Island, a peaceful oasis rich in natural beauty and history. The island offers a variety of walking trails amidst its verdant meadows and along its rocky coastline. The panoramic view of the surrounding sea and the mainland is worth the trip alone.

The island is also home to some historic buildings, including the oldest stone house in Iceland, built in 1755. There's also a beautiful sculpture by American artist Richard Serra, entitled "The Milestones". Consisting of nine pairs of basalt columns spread across the island, the installation highlights the unique character of Videy and the surrounding environment.

Videy Island is the perfect day trip for those seeking to escape the city's hustle and bustle. Don't forget to check the ferry timetable and weather conditions before you head out. While there are no shops on the island, there's a small restaurant in the old stone house, where you can sample some traditional Icelandic dishes.

Reykjavik Cuisine

Iceland's capital city, Reykjavik, is a food lover's paradise, offering a fantastic mix of traditional Icelandic cuisine and international flavors. From high-end dining establishments to quaint bistros and trendy food halls, Reykjavik's culinary scene is as varied as it is delicious.

Fish and lamb are staples in Icelandic cuisine, often served with locally grown vegetables like potatoes and kale. For those adventurous eaters, trying traditional dishes such as "hákarl" (fermented shark), "harðfiskur" (dried fish), or "svið" (singed sheep's head) is a must. For the sweet tooth, don't miss out on trying "skyr", a creamy dairy product similar to yogurt.

For a more casual dining experience, head over to one of the city's food halls, like Hlemmur Mathöll or Grandi Mathöll, where you'll find a variety of food stalls serving everything from Vietnamese street food to Icelandic fish and chips. Another popular option is the famous Bæjarins Beztu Pylsur hot dog stand, a favorite among locals and tourists alike. Eating your way through Reykjavik is an adventure in itself and a fantastic way to experience Iceland's evolving culinary landscape.

Final Thoughts

Exploring Reykjavik is like embarking on a thrilling treasure hunt, where you uncover gems at every turn. This city is teeming with cultural riches, captivating history, gastronomical delights, and experiences that touch the soul. Reykjavik, despite its size, packs a hefty punch and will surely leave an indelible mark on your travel memory bank.

Another spot worth mentioning is the Perlan, a remarkable building with a revolving glass dome that offers a panoramic view of the city. You could also visit the Geothermal Beach at Nautholsvik for a quick dip in warm waters, even in colder months! Reykjavik is also a gateway to the stunning landscapes of Iceland. Several tour operators offer day trips to the Golden Circle, South Coast, and the Snæfellsnes Peninsula, making Reykjavik an ideal base for your Icelandic adventure.

Beyond its physical attractions, what makes Reykjavik truly special is its welcoming people, who wear their hearts on their sleeves. Their warmth and hospitality amplify the beauty of this Nordic city. Don't be surprised if you find yourself in a friendly conversation with a local at a coffee shop or a pub. These interactions often lead to insider tips and fascinating stories that you won't find in any guidebook.

Don't rush your visit to Reykjavik. Take your time to wander around, soak in the city's vibe, savor its food, and immerse yourself in its culture. This approach will lead to a deeper appreciation of the city's charm and character. After all, the beauty of travel lies in experiences and connections, not just in ticking off a checklist.

As we proceed in this guide, we'll be taking you on a journey through Iceland, beyond its capital city. The breathtaking landscapes, extraordinary natural wonders, and unique cultural experiences that await will be something to look forward to. So grab your warm clothes, your sense of adventure, and let's continue this Icelandic journey together.

30　　　　　　　　　　　　　　　　　　ICELAND TRAVEL GUIDE

CHAPTER 2: GOLDEN CIRCLE 31

CHAPTER 2:
Golden Circle

The Golden Circle, a popular travel route in South Iceland, provides a snapshot of what makes Iceland so unique: its dramatic landscapes, geological wonders, and a deep-rooted history that has shaped the nation's identity. This roughly 300-kilometer loop from Reykjavik encompasses three main stops: Thingvellir National Park, the Geysir Geothermal Area, and Gullfoss Waterfall. But there's more to the Golden Circle than these headline acts, and as you follow this route, you'll discover the lesser-known gems that make the journey as rewarding as the destination itself.

Embarking on a Golden Circle tour is like stepping into a realm where nature has pulled out all the stops. You'll witness the aftermath of volcanic activity, marvel at gushing waterfalls, see geysers explode before your eyes, and get a feel of the earth's raw power. Whether you're driving yourself or opting for a guided tour, the Golden Circle provides a compact yet compelling exploration of Iceland's natural beauty and fascinating geology. But the Golden Circle isn't just about nature's spectacle. It's also a journey through history, a pilgrimage that takes you to the cradle of Icelandic democracy and through a landscape shaped by a millennia of human and volcanic activity. The Golden Circle route is easily accessible and offers a wide range of activities for all kinds of travelers. From leisurely sightseeing and hearty Icelandic meals to horseback riding and bathing in geothermal waters, there's something for everyone.

Thingvellir National Park

Located on the shores of Iceland's largest lake, Þingvallavatn, Thingvellir National Park is a place of great natural beauty and historical significance. It's a UNESCO World Heritage site and the birthplace of the Althingi, the world's oldest surviving parliament, established in 930 AD. This is where chieftains from all over Iceland used to gather to discuss legal matters, make laws, and settle disputes.

Thingvellir is also an important site for geology enthusiasts. The park lies in a rift valley created by the separation of the North American and Eurasian tectonic plates. Visitors can walk between these two continents along the Almannagjá fault. You can also see Þingvallavatn, the largest natural lake in Iceland, as well as various rivers, waterfalls, and fissures within the park.

An unmissable activity in Thingvellir is snorkeling or diving in Silfra, a fissure filled with crystal-clear glacial water. Here, you can touch two continents simultaneously while enjoying visibility up to 100 meters. Remember to dress warmly and prepare for a truly unique underwater adventure.

Geysir Geothermal Area

The Geysir Geothermal Area, located in the Haukadalur Valley, is a hotbed of geothermal activity. Named after the Great Geysir, which is now mostly dormant, this area is a dynamic display of nature's power. The star of the show today is Strokkur, a geyser that erupts every 5-10 minutes, shooting water and steam up to 30 meters into the air.

A walk around the Geysir Geothermal Area reveals boiling mud pits, smaller geysers, and colorful mineral deposits. An onsite geology museum offers insight into the geothermal activity and the area's history. Also, a nearby restaurant and gift shop make this a convenient stop for a meal or souvenir shopping.

Despite its raw and untamed nature, the Geysir Geothermal Area is well-marked and safe for visitors. However, it's important to stick to the paths, as the ground can be hot and unstable. And don't forget your camera; capturing the moment of eruption is an experience not to be missed!

Gullfoss Waterfall

Gullfoss, or the 'Golden Falls', is one of Iceland's most iconic and beloved waterfalls, known for its sheer power and beauty. Fed by the Langjökull glacier, the Hvítá river cascades down two tiers into a deep canyon, creating a spectacular sight. On sunny days, the mist from the waterfall creates rainbows, adding to the allure of the location.

The falls can be admired from several viewpoints, each offering a unique perspective. The upper deck provides a panoramic view, while a walk down a staircase leads to a lower deck, where you can feel the mist of the waterfall on your face. In winter, Gullfoss can freeze into a stunning ice sculpture, while summer brings vibrant hues of green surrounding the falls.

When visiting Gullfoss, make sure to wear appropriate clothing, as the mist from the waterfall can make the area quite damp. Also, tread carefully around the site, particularly in winter, when the paths can be icy.

Kerid Crater Lake

Kerið, a volcanic crater lake located in the Grímsnes area, is a lesser-known yet fascinating stop on the Golden Circle route. Around 3,000 years old, Kerið is one part of a group of volcanic hills called Tjarnarhólar. Its steep walls, made of red volcanic rock, dramatically contrast with the azure-blue water filling the crater and the lush green moss that blankets the surroundings. Visitors can walk around the top rim of the crater, which offers panoramic views of the vibrant colors. There's also a path leading down to the lakeshore, allowing you a closer look at the brilliantly hued water. Kerið isn't as grand as other Golden Circle sights, but its striking colors make it a photographer's dream. Remember, the site has an entrance fee, but it's minimal and goes towards maintaining the site. The walking path can be a bit steep, so it's recommended to wear good shoes when visiting Kerið.

Faxi Waterfall

Just off the main Golden Circle route lies the charming Faxi waterfall. Also known as Vatnsleysufoss, this waterfall is less known compared to its grand neighbor Gullfoss but is just as worthy of a visit. The waterfall is wide and cascades beautifully over a 7-meter drop into a pretty pool below.

Faxi is surrounded by a peaceful countryside, making it a delightful spot for a picnic. There's also a salmon ladder constructed near the waterfall, aiming to assist salmon travel upstream during the breeding season – a fascinating sight if you're visiting in the right season.

Though not as powerful or dramatic as other Icelandic waterfalls, Faxi's charm lies in its tranquillity and beauty. A small parking fee is charged at the waterfall, which helps maintain the facilities, including the picnic area and the walking path leading to the waterfall.

Secret Lagoon in Flúðir

The Secret Lagoon, or Gamla Laugin, nestled in the small village of Flúðir, is a geothermal hot spring that offers a slice of tranquil Icelandic bliss. Dating back to 1891, it's one of the oldest swimming pools in Iceland, with its warm waters maintaining a steady temperature of 38-40°C (100-104°F) year-round. Unlike the larger, more commercialized hot springs, the Secret Lagoon provides an authentic and relaxing geothermal spa experience.
Visiting the Secret Lagoon is akin to stepping into a different world. The steam rising from the water surface creates a mystical atmosphere, while the surrounding greenery and small geysers that erupt every few minutes enhance the sense of natural wonder. Take your time to unwind in the therapeutic waters and soak up the incredible landscape views.
Visiting during winter may even offer a chance to witness the Northern Lights while floating in the warm water. Just remember to bring your swimsuit and towel, although they can be rented on-site. Lockers are available for your belongings. Booking your visit in advance is advised, especially during peak tourist season.

Efstidalur II (Farm and Restaurant)

Efstidalur II, a family-owned farm in the Laugarvatn region, provides a delightful food and farming experience within the

Golden Circle route. The farm, which dates back to 1750, introduces visitors to traditional Icelandic farming practices while also serving delicious, home-made farm-to-table meals.

At Efstidalur II, you can see how the food is produced right on the farm. The place is particularly known for its ice cream barn, where visitors can watch cows being milked while enjoying ice cream made from their milk. The restaurant offers a variety of dishes, but the homemade burgers using the farm's beef are a crowd favourite.

Apart from the culinary delights, visitors can enjoy horse riding tours around the scenic farm. It's a fantastic way to explore the beautiful countryside and get close to the famous Icelandic horses. Remember, as this place is popular, it might be worth making a restaurant reservation in advance, especially during summer.

Icelandic Horses

One of the unique features of Iceland's landscape is its native horse breed, known as the Icelandic horse. Small, sturdy, and with a gentle demeanor, these horses are beloved by locals and visitors alike. They are unique for their tölt, a smooth gait that provides a comfortable ride over the rugged Icelandic terrain.

A horseback riding tour is one of the best ways to experience the Golden Circle's breathtaking landscapes, whether it's a short trip around a farm or a full-day excursion into the countryside. Many tour operators offer riding tours suitable for all skill levels, so even if you've never ridden a horse before, you can still enjoy this experience.

Remember to dress warmly and wear long pants and sturdy shoes for your ride. Also, due to strict regulations protecting the breed from diseases, it's not allowed to bring used riding gear into the country. Most tour operators will provide you with all necessary riding equipment.

Laugarvatn Fontana

Nestled on the shores of Lake Laugarvatn, the Fontana Geothermal Baths offers a sublime experience of Iceland's natural geothermal power. This spa, built directly over a hot spring, offers visitors a chance to relax and rejuvenate in warm geothermal pools and natural steam rooms. The steam is produced by hot spring water that simmers directly beneath the ground.

The bath's location offers mesmerizing views of the surrounding landscape, especially the serene lake and the distant mountains. There's something truly magical about unwinding in the warm water while taking in such breathtaking scenery. Don't forget to dip in the cold lake water; it's said to be invigorating and good for your health.

It's recommended to bring your own towel and swimsuit, although they can be rented on-site. Refreshments are available at the cafe, including traditional Icelandic rye bread baked in the geothermal sand. If you're traveling during winter, the late hours might reward you with a display of the Northern Lights over the lake.

Flora and Fauna

One of the most delightful aspects of traveling the Golden Circle is the chance to encounter Iceland's unique flora and fauna. The area's diverse habitats host a variety of wildlife, including the hardy Icelandic horse, often seen grazing in fields along the route. Birdwatchers, too, will be thrilled by the numerous species that inhabit the region, especially near water bodies like Gullfoss waterfall.

Flora in this area is just as enchanting, though it tends to be more visible in the warmer months. From vibrant mosses and lichens to resilient shrubs and flowering plants, the Golden Circle's vegetation tells a story of survival and adaptability in harsh conditions. While wandering the Golden Circle, remember to respect the wildlife and plants, maintaining a safe distance, and leaving no trace.

Historical Significance

The Golden Circle doesn't just offer natural wonders; it's also a journey through Iceland's rich history. Thingvellir National Park, for instance, isn't just a geological marvel; it's also the site of Althing, the world's oldest surviving parliament established in 930 AD. It was here that chieftains from all over the country would meet to settle disputes, pass laws, and make significant decisions. Each location along the route has its own historical tales, often intertwined with the sagas - the historical narratives about early Icelandic history. Learning about these stories adds depth to your experience, making each site more than just a beautiful vista. Make sure to take some time to delve into the area's historical narratives, either through guided tours or personal research. You could add the Flora and Fauna section after "Secret Lagoon in Flúðir," to provide readers with a more encompassing view of what they can expect along the route, and the Historical Significance section after "Thingvellir National Park," to give readers a deeper understanding of the area's cultural importance.

Exploring the Golden Circle by Night

Experiencing the Golden Circle by night presents a new perspective on Iceland's magnificent landscapes. The twilight adds a layer of mystery and enchantment to the sites, especially in winter when the chance to see the Northern Lights is higher. Imagine witnessing the Geysir erupt or the Gullfoss waterfall illuminated under the starry sky, it's a truly mesmerizing sight. There are various tour operators offering night tours around the Golden Circle, complete with expert guides who can provide insightful commentary on the Icelandic folklore associated with these sites. While exploring the Golden Circle by night, ensure you dress warmly and wear sturdy footwear as the temperatures drop significantly.

If you're driving yourself, be cautious as the road conditions can be challenging at night, especially during winter. Also, it's recommended to check the aurora forecast before planning a night tour to increase your chances of witnessing the stunning Northern Lights display.

Final Thoughts

The Golden Circle route is more than just a checklist of tourist sites; it's a journey into the heart of Iceland, offering a glimpse into its geology, history, culture, and culinary delights. To truly appreciate its beauty, don't rush your visit. Each location has its unique charm and deserves time for exploration and admiration.

While major sites like Thingvellir National Park, Gullfoss, and Geysir are must-visits, remember to also explore the lesser-known treasures. Places like the Secret Lagoon in Flúðir or the Efstidalur II farm can provide intimate and authentic Icelandic experiences.

Also, try to be flexible with your schedule. Weather in Iceland can be unpredictable and might require you to rearrange your plans. Always check the weather and road conditions before setting out for the day. It's also beneficial to have a plan B, like a local museum or restaurant, in case the weather turns against you.

Keep in mind that while the Golden Circle is accessible year-round, each season offers a different experience. The summer months promise longer days, greener landscapes, and more wildlife, while the winter unveils a starkly beautiful snowy landscape and a chance to see the Northern Lights.

We hope this guide helps you plan your trip to the Golden Circle and inspires you to delve deeper into what Iceland has to offer. Remember, this is just the beginning. There's so much more to see, explore, and experience in this remarkable country. So, keep reading, keep planning, and prepare for an unforgettable Icelandic adventure.

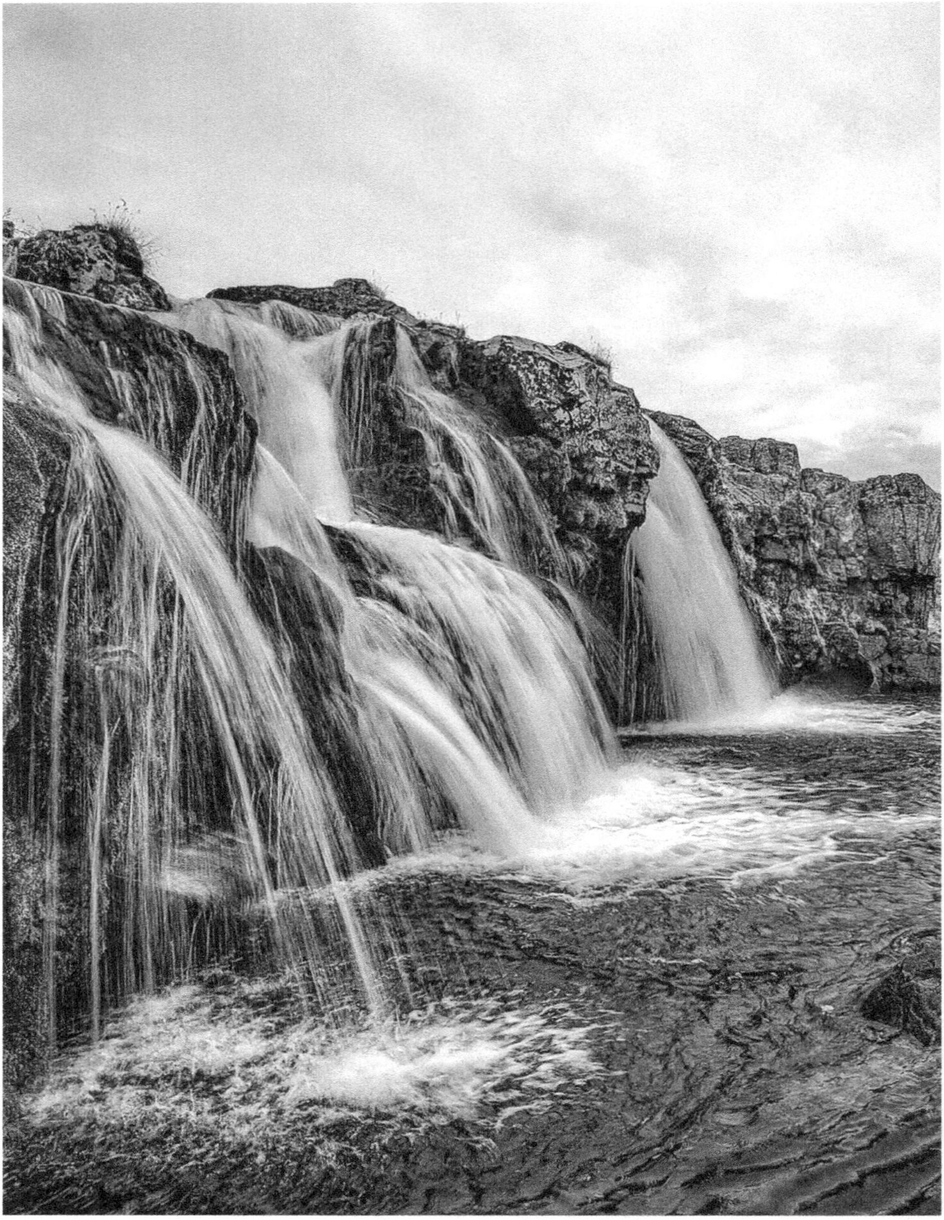

CHAPTER 3: SOUTH COAST 45

CHAPTER 3:
South Coast

The South Coast of Iceland, a spellbinding stretch of land known for its scenic diversity and natural splendor, is a must-see for any intrepid traveler. It is a region where each bend in the road reveals new wonders, from thundering waterfalls and picturesque villages to black sand beaches and glittering glacier lagoons. Journeying through the South Coast isn't just a trip; it's an immersion into an otherworldly landscape that will leave you awe-struck at every turn.

This chapter will guide you through the remarkable sights and experiences the South Coast has to offer. It's important to note that while the area's raw beauty is breathtaking, it also demands respect and caution. Always heed local safety guidelines, especially when dealing with natural elements like glaciers, beaches, and waterfalls. The South Coast, with its ever-changing weather and powerful natural forces, serves as a humbling reminder of nature's supremacy.

With careful planning, respect for the environment, and an adventurous spirit, exploring the South Coast can be an unforgettable journey. From the powerful sprays of Seljalandsfoss and Skógafoss waterfalls to the tranquil beauty of Jökulsárlón Glacier Lagoon, every experience will be etched in your memory. So, strap in for a ride of a lifetime as we embark on this journey through one of Iceland's most stunning regions.

Seljalandsfoss Waterfall

Seljalandsfoss, one of the most iconic waterfalls on the South Coast, is renowned for its dramatic beauty. Cascading from a height of about 60 meters, the waterfall's most distinctive feature is the cave behind the water curtain, which allows visitors to walk behind the falls for a unique perspective. The sight of the water tumbling from overhead, with the sunlight creating rainbows in the mist, is a truly spectacular experience.

The ground can be slippery, especially in wet weather, so be sure to wear sturdy, waterproof shoes. It's also advisable to have a waterproof jacket as the spray from the waterfall can get you pretty wet, especially if you're venturing behind it. Despite the potential for getting a little damp, the unique view from behind the falls is something you won't want to miss.

Even if you're not one for getting up close and personal with the falls, the surrounding meadows offer a serene spot for picnicking, bird watching, or simply basking in the beauty of the landscape. Remember to respect the environment by not littering and staying on marked trails.

Skógafoss Waterfall

Another breathtaking sight on the South Coast is Skógafoss, one of the largest and most beautiful waterfalls in Iceland. With a drop of 60 meters and a width of 25 meters, it's a powerful spectacle. On sunny days, the spray from the waterfall often creates a stunning rainbow, making for incredible photo opportunities.

At Skógafoss, you can experience the waterfall from both its foot and its top. A staircase on the right side of the waterfall leads up to an observation platform, offering a panoramic view over the falls and surrounding landscape. It's a bit of a climb, but the view from the top is well worth the effort. Be sure to hold onto the handrails, as the steps can be wet and slippery.

Near the waterfall, you'll find facilities like a café, toilets, and a camping site. If you're interested in learning more about the region's history and folklore, the Skógar Museum, located just a short distance from the falls, is worth a visit. Local legend has it that the first Viking settler in the area buried a treasure in a cave behind the waterfall. While you're unlikely to find any gold, the beauty of Skógafoss is a treasure in its own right.

Reynisfjara Black Sand Beach

Reynisfjara, known for its striking black sand, is a beach unlike any other. The contrast of the dark volcanic sand against the crashing waves of the North Atlantic is a sight to behold. The beach's dramatic basalt columns, sea stacks, and caves also add to its unique allure. It's no wonder Reynisfjara has been rated one of the most beautiful non-tropical beaches in the world.

However, it's essential to remember that Reynisfjara is as dangerous as it is beautiful. The beach is known for its "sneaker waves": suddenly powerful and high waves that can pull unaware visitors out to sea. Always keep a safe distance from the water, never turn your back to the waves, and stay clear of the basalt columns where waves can crash in unexpectedly.

Near the beach, you'll find a café where you can warm up with a cup of coffee or hot chocolate and some traditional Icelandic pastries. Be sure to also visit the charming village of Vík, which is just a short drive away and offers further dining and shopping options.

Vik Village

Vík í Mýrdal, generally known as Vík, is the southernmost village in Iceland. With a population of around 300, it's a small but charming settlement that serves as an essential service center for those traveling on the South Coast. Surrounded by beautiful high bird cliffs, Vík is an excellent spot for bird watching, especially for puffins, which nest there during the summer.

The village itself offers several services including a supermarket, a gas station, restaurants, and a wool factory outlet selling traditional Icelandic clothing. It's a great place to stop for a meal, fill up your tank, or pick up any supplies you might need for your journey.

Be sure to take a walk through the village to the local church. Located on a hill, it provides a fantastic view of the village and the surrounding landscape, including the iconic Reynisdrangar sea stacks. The church is also historically significant as it is one of the few high grounds that villagers would evacuate to during volcanic eruptions.

Dyrhólaey Peninsula

The Dyrhólaey Peninsula is a small promontory located near the village of Vík. It's renowned for its stunning views of the South Coast, its massive arch that the sea has carved into the cliff, and its diverse birdlife, including the endearing puffins. From atop the cliffs of Dyrhólaey, you can see for miles, with views of the black sand beaches, the village of Vík, and the Mýrdalsjökull glacier.

Dyrhólaey is reachable by car, and there are two parking lots at different levels. The higher one offers more expansive views but requires a 4x4 vehicle to reach. The lower one is accessible to all cars and is just a short walk from the lighthouse, which is a must-see while you're there.

While visiting Dyrhólaey, be sure to respect the wildlife, particularly during nesting season, when certain areas may be closed off to protect the birds. The weather can also be quite windy, so dress accordingly and be careful near cliff edges.

Solheimajokull Glacier

The Solheimajokull Glacier is a breathtaking icy wonderland that's part of the larger Mýrdalsjökull glacier. It's a favorite among adventurous travelers because it offers excellent opportunities for hiking and ice climbing. The glacier's surface is a stunning mix of white snow, deep blue ice, and black ash from volcanic eruptions.

There are guided tours that offer the equipment and safety briefings needed for a glacier hike or climb. It's not advised to explore glaciers alone due to their ever-changing nature and potential hazards, such as crevasses and falling ice. A guided tour will also provide fascinating insights about the glacier's geology, its formation, and the impact of climate change.

While at Solheimajokull, don't miss the nearby Skogafoss and Seljalandsfoss waterfalls, as well as the Solheimasandur Plane Wreck, a hauntingly beautiful site of a crashed US Navy airplane.

Jokulsarlon Glacier Lagoon

Next up is the Jokulsarlon Glacier Lagoon, one of Iceland's natural crown jewels. This large glacial lake is filled with massive icebergs that have broken off from the nearby Breiðamerkurjökull glacier. Seeing these floating ice giants up close is a truly humbling experience.

During the summer, boat tours take visitors among the sculptural icebergs. You might also spot seals which frequently swim in the lagoon or rest on the ice. During the winter, when conditions allow, it's possible to explore the stunning blue ice caves that form in the glacier above the lagoon.

Just across the road from the lagoon is Diamond Beach, where smaller icebergs wash ashore and sparkle like diamonds on the black sand. Both the lagoon and the beach offer some of the most unique and photogenic landscapes in Iceland.

Diamond Beach

Diamond Beach is a magnificent strip of black sand adorned with chunks of glacial ice. The ice washes up on the beach after breaking away from the nearby Jokulsarlon Glacier Lagoon and being carried out to sea. These ice pieces can range from the size of a small pebble to the size of a car, and their sparkling clear to blue tinted appearance against the black sand makes for an incredibly surreal and beautiful landscape.

The best time to visit Diamond Beach is at sunrise or sunset, when the low sun illuminates the ice chunks, making them glisten like real diamonds. It's a photographer's dream come true, but remember to be careful and keep a safe distance from the water, as the waves can be unpredictable and powerful.

There are no facilities at Diamond Beach, so be sure to bring any essentials like food and water with you. And don't forget to stop by the Jokulsarlon Glacier Lagoon – it's right across the road and not to be missed on any trip along Iceland's South Coast.

South Coast by Night

Exploring the South Coast by night opens up a new world of magic and mystery. The main attraction is the chance to witness the Northern Lights, also known as the Aurora Borealis. This natural light display, created by solar particles entering the Earth's atmosphere, paints the night sky with hues of green, pink, and sometimes even red and purple.

The South Coast's rural setting away from the light pollution of urban areas makes it an ideal spot for Northern Lights hunting. However, sightings depend on solar activity and clear skies, so they are not guaranteed. Late fall to early spring are the best times to try and catch them.

In the summertime, when the sun barely sets, you can experience the natural phenomenon of the midnight sun. This provides extended daylight hours, great for late-night hikes or drives. It's a surreal experience to see the landscape bathed in a soft, golden light at midnight.

Day Trip to Vestmannaeyjar

If you're exploring the South Coast, consider making a day trip to Vestmannaeyjar, also known as the Westman Islands. This archipelago is located just off the coast, and the main island, Heimaey, is a short ferry ride away.

Heimaey boasts a rich history and stunning natural beauty. Visit the Eldheimar Museum to learn about the 1973 volcanic eruption that caused the island's residents to evacuate. The island is also known for its abundant bird life, including puffins, so don't miss a visit to Stórhöfði, a great spot for birdwatching.

Other activities in Vestmannaeyjar include hiking around the island's numerous trails, exploring its sea caves by boat, and golfing at one of Iceland's most picturesque courses.

South Coast Cuisine

A journey around the South Coast is also a journey of culinary delights. As with the rest of the country, lamb and seafood are prominent in South Coast cuisine. Visit a local restaurant and try the Icelandic fish soup or the traditional Plokkfiskur, a creamy fish and potato dish.

Local farms often serve homemade ice cream, skyr (a traditional Icelandic yogurt), and cheese. Make sure to stop by Efstidalur II, a farm in the Golden Circle area, for an ice cream tasting while watching the cows through a glass window.

And if you're an adventurous eater, stop at the village of Vik for a taste of Hákarl, fermented shark, which is a traditional Icelandic delicacy. Just a heads up, it's an acquired taste!

Final Thoughts

There's no denying the South Coast's magnetic allure, as it seamlessly intertwines nature's raw power and delicate beauty. It's a place that encourages adventure and rewards curiosity, making it a must-see destination for anyone visiting Iceland.

If you find yourself with extra time, consider exploring the lesser-known attractions like Fjaðrárgljúfur, a stunning and dramatic canyon a short drive from the ring road. Its green mossy walls and winding river provide breathtaking vistas, particularly in the summer months.

For a truly immersive South Coast experience, why not try a few nights in one of the many camping grounds or cottages dotted along the coast? They offer a cost-effective and unique accommodation option. Imagine waking up to the sound of crashing waves or going to sleep under a starlit sky, with the ethereal glow of the Northern Lights dancing overhead.

Remember, the weather in this region can change rapidly, so always dress in layers, even in summer, and check weather conditions regularly, particularly if you're planning to hike or camp. Respect the environment, stay on marked trails, and never underestimate the power of nature, particularly the ocean's currents and waves.

Also, keep in mind that while major landmarks usually have visitor facilities, in more remote areas, amenities can be sparse. So, always have some snacks, water, and a full tank of gas when embarking on your day trips.

In closing, the South Coast's enchanting landscapes and diverse activities offer visitors an unforgettable experience, each one unique to the season, time of day, and weather. Whether it's the sense of tranquility from watching a sunset paint the sky behind a waterfall, the thrill of hiking a glacier, or the awe of watching the Northern Lights, the South Coast is sure to leave you with lasting memories and stories to share. It truly is an embodiment of Iceland's natural charm.

Next, we venture into the Westfjords, a region less visited but equally mesmerizing. So, refill your coffee mug or grab another pint, as our Icelandic journey continues.

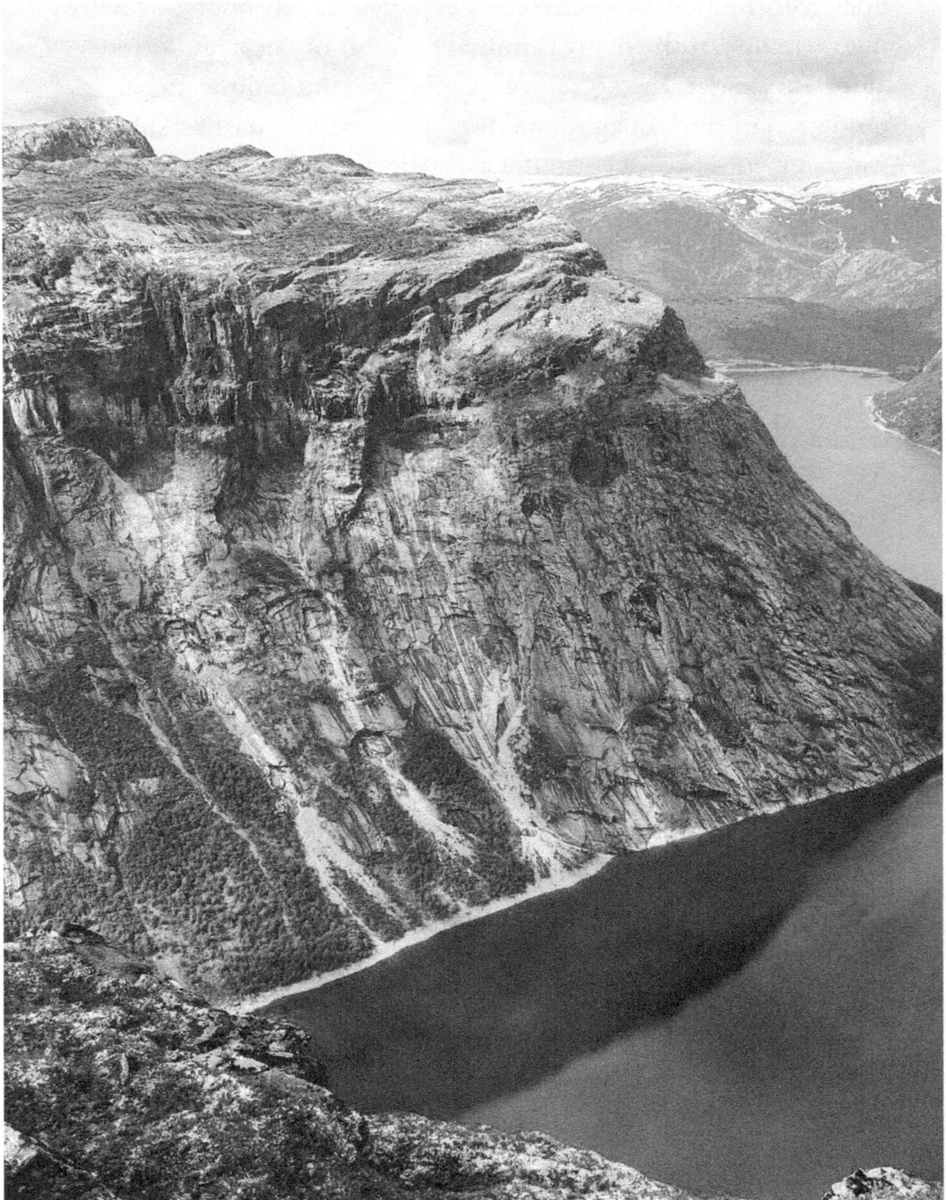

CHAPTER 4: WESTFJORDS

CHAPTER 4:
Westfjords

Anchored in the northwest corner of Iceland, the Westfjords region is often overlooked by many visitors due to its remote location. However, those willing to venture off the beaten path will discover a world of untamed landscapes, abundant wildlife, and a timeless sense of tranquility.

The region boasts a rugged coastline dotted with tiny fishing villages, steep mountains that plunge into the sea, and serene fjords that meander inland. Here, you'll find one of the country's most dramatic landscapes, where nature has been left largely untouched by man. While the journey to reach the Westfjords can be challenging, especially during the winter months, the rewards are well worth it.

Your adventure in the Westfjords may lead you to the precipice of towering sea cliffs, the base of powerful waterfalls, the edge of vast stretches of red sand, or the heart of small towns with rich histories. This chapter will guide you through some of the Westfjords' highlights, offering practical advice to make your journey as enriching as possible. So buckle up and get ready for an unforgettable trip through one of Iceland's most awe-inspiring regions.

Dynjandi Waterfall

One of the most captivating sights in the Westfjords is the Dynjandi waterfall. Also known as Fjallfoss, this majestic cascade is a series of seven waterfalls that collectively reach a height of about 100 meters. The most distinctive and largest of these is Dynjandi, which means "thunderous" in Icelandic, an apt name given the cascade's powerful roar.

The waterfall's striking feature is its form, shaped like a large bridal veil, getting wider as the water descends down the mountain. The view from the bottom is impressive, but the short hike to the top provides a more up-close experience and offers stunning vistas of the fjord below.

Despite its remote location, the site is equipped with facilities such as parking and restrooms. Be sure to wear sturdy footwear for the hike, and remember to respect the environment by staying on marked paths. The best time to visit is during the summer months when the waterfall is at its most powerful, and the road conditions are generally more favorable.

Latrabjarg Cliffs

Venture to the westernmost point of Iceland, and you'll find the Latrabjarg Cliffs, a stunning sea cliff that stretches over 14 kilometers and reaches up to 440 meters at its highest point. Known as Europe's largest bird cliff, it's a paradise for bird watchers, as it's home to millions of seabirds, especially during the nesting season in summer.

Puffins are the main draw here. Unlike in other parts of Iceland, they are quite tame and allow visitors to get relatively close, making it a dream spot for photographers. However, caution is needed as the cliff edges can be unstable, so always keep a safe distance.

Visitors should note that while the cliffs are free to visit, they are quite remote and require a considerable drive on gravel roads. Be prepared for a longer journey, and it might be best to plan for a full day's trip. Don't forget to bring your binoculars for the best birdwatching experience, and always respect the wildlife by keeping a reasonable distance and avoiding any sudden movements that may startle the birds.

Raudasandur Beach

When you think of Iceland, a beach might not be the first thing that comes to mind. However, Raudasandur Beach, or "Red Sand Beach," is an exception that will leave you pleasantly surprised. This expansive coastline is famous for its unique reddish-pink sand that contrasts with the blue Atlantic waves, a stark departure from the black sand beaches found elsewhere in the country.

This serene landscape is complemented by a dramatic backdrop of steep cliffs, making for a picturesque and peaceful visit. Wildlife enthusiasts will also appreciate the opportunity to spot seals basking on the shore, especially during the summer months.

Access to Raudasandur can be a little tricky, with a narrow and winding road leading to the beach, but the exceptional scenery awaiting you is well worth the drive. Remember, Icelandic weather can be unpredictable, so dress in layers and carry waterproof gear. Also, bring your own refreshments as there are no facilities nearby. As always, leave no trace behind to preserve this beautiful place for future visitors.

Isafjordur Town

Nestled among towering mountains and beautiful fjords, Isafjordur is the largest town in the Westfjords region. Despite its small size, the town brims with charm and provides a fascinating glimpse into Icelandic life off the beaten path.

Wander around the town, and you'll find a collection of old timber houses dating back to the 18th century, lending a quaint, historic feel. The town is also home to a harbor where you'll see fishing boats come and go, underlining the importance of fishing to the local economy.

There are several cafes and restaurants where you can enjoy fresh local seafood, and small shops featuring local handicrafts. For a bit of culture, consider a visit to the Westfjords Heritage Museum, which gives insight into the region's maritime history. When planning your visit, remember that facilities and services in the town might be limited compared to what's available in larger cities like Reykjavik, but the welcoming spirit of the locals and the beautiful surroundings make for a memorable stay.

Hornstrandir Nature Reserve

The Hornstrandir Nature Reserve is the northernmost peninsula in the Westfjords and is a must-visit for nature enthusiasts. This untouched wilderness area is completely uninhabited and is characterized by dramatic cliffs, lush valleys, diverse flora and fauna, and picturesque hiking trails.

A haven for wildlife, Hornstrandir is the perfect place to spot Arctic foxes, who have no fear of humans due to the lack of hunting in the reserve. During the summer, the cliffs become home to a wide variety of bird species, making it an excellent destination for birdwatching.

The reserve can only be reached by boat during the summer months, with daily departures from Isafjordur. There are no services or facilities in Hornstrandir, so visitors must bring all their necessities and be prepared for unpredictable weather. Camping is allowed, but remember to respect the environment by following the "leave no trace" principles. Hornstrandir is a unique adventure that brings you into intimate contact with Iceland's unspoiled beauty.

Hot Springs of Westfjords

Nothing quite encapsulates the Icelandic experience like taking a dip in a natural hot spring, and Westfjords has plenty to offer. The geothermal activity beneath Iceland's rugged surface creates natural hot tubs that are perfect for relaxation.

In the remote Westfjords, these hot springs are often less crowded than their counterparts in the more tourist-heavy regions, giving you the opportunity to soak in peace. One such location is the Reykjafjarðarlaug Hot Pool, a geothermal hot tub with an unbeatable view of the surrounding fjord.

While the hot springs are open year-round, the best time to visit is in winter when you can potentially enjoy a soak while gazing at the Northern Lights. However, always remember to respect the local environment, keep noise levels down, and clean up after yourself. It's also essential to check the temperature before entering, as some hot springs can be dangerously hot.

Westfjords by Night

When the sun sets, Westfjords transforms into a world of enchanting beauty. The region's remote location and lack of light pollution make it one of the best places in Iceland to witness the Northern Lights. Watching this breathtaking natural phenomenon dance across the sky is an experience that you will cherish for a lifetime.

If you're visiting in summer, the nights are bright, and the midnight sun gives you plenty of extra hours to explore. This is a perfect time for late-night hikes, providing a different perspective on the landscapes that you won't get during the daytime.

During your nighttime adventures, always prioritize safety. Keep an eye on the weather conditions, dress warmly, and let someone know your plans. It's also recommended to join a guided Northern Lights tour, as local guides know the best viewing spots and can help ensure a safe and enjoyable experience.

Road Trip Around Westfjords

Exploring Westfjords by car is one of the best ways to appreciate the region's majestic landscapes. The winding roads take you through a diverse range of scenery, from towering mountains and deep fjords to cascading waterfalls and charming little towns.

While Route 60, known as the Westfjords Way, is a highlight with its dramatic cliffs and sweeping views, the more adventurous might prefer the lesser-known roads that lead to remote areas like the Hornstrandir Nature Reserve.

Before you set off, ensure your vehicle is suited to the region's challenging roads—four-wheel drives are recommended. Also, check weather and road conditions, as sudden changes can make driving hazardous. And finally, take your time, make frequent stops to soak in the views, and remember that in Iceland, the journey is just as important as the destination.

Boat Tours from Isafjordur

Isafjordur, the biggest town in the Westfjords, is the perfect starting point for memorable boat tours. These excursions take you out into the stunning fjords, where you'll witness breathtaking landscapes, towering sea cliffs, and, if you're lucky, an array of marine life.
Whale watching is a popular option, with tours often spotting humpback whales, white-beaked dolphins, and even orcas. Bird enthusiasts, meanwhile, will appreciate the puffin tours that take you to their nesting areas on the nearby cliffs.
When choosing a boat tour, always consider the weather and sea conditions. Make sure to dress warmly, even in summer, as it can get cold out on the water. Don't forget your camera to capture the unique experiences that these boat tours provide.

Wildlife Spotting in Westfjords

In addition to its spectacular landscapes, Westfjords is also a haven for wildlife. The region's remote location and rugged terrains have created perfect habitats for a variety of animals, adding another exciting aspect to your visit.
Birdwatchers will be delighted with the area's richness in bird species. Hornstrandir Nature Reserve, for instance, is a nesting site for countless seabirds, including puffins and the Arctic tern.

On land, keep an eye out for Arctic foxes—the only terrestrial mammal native to Iceland.

Respect for the wildlife is of utmost importance when you're out exploring. Always observe animals from a distance, never feed wild animals, and make sure not to disturb nesting birds. Joining a guided wildlife tour can be a good way to learn more about the local fauna while minimizing the impact on their natural habitats.

Westfjords Cuisine

The Westfjords' cuisine is a reflection of the region's close relationship with the sea. Freshly caught seafood, from Atlantic cod to Arctic char, features heavily on local menus, prepared using traditional methods passed down through generations.

In Isafjordur, there are several restaurants serving dishes made from local ingredients, often with a modern twist. A popular specialty is the traditional Icelandic fish soup, a hearty and delicious bowl filled with fresh fish and root vegetables.

If you're self-catering, the local fish market is a great place to find the day's catch. And, if you're lucky enough to be visiting during berry picking season, the Westfjords' countryside is full of crowberries and bilberries waiting to be harvested. As always, try to eat at local, independently owned eateries when possible, to support local businesses and get the most authentic experience.

Final Thoughts

We've covered a lot of ground here in the Westfjords, but this remote and rugged region has so much more to offer. Picture vast landscapes dotted with quaint villages, where time seems to have stood still. There's an adventure around every corner here, whether it's hiking through unspoiled wilderness or soaking in a hidden hot spring.

Driving in the Westfjords can be a challenge, with winding gravel roads clinging to steep cliffs. However, the scenery that unfolds before you is more than worth it. Remember to take your time, plan your route, and always check the weather and road conditions before setting off. And don't hesitate to ask locals for advice—they're usually happy to share their knowledge and may even recommend some hidden gems that are off the beaten track.

One such place could be the Strandir Coast, an isolated and enchanting part of the Westfjords that we haven't touched upon. Known for its deep-rooted folklore and enchanting landscapes, it's a place where you can truly feel one with nature. While you're there, be sure to visit the Museum of Icelandic Witchcraft and Sorcery in Hólmavík for an insight into Iceland's mystical past.

You'll notice that the Westfjords is less touristy than other parts of Iceland, giving you a more intimate and authentic experience. This is a place where you can fully immerse yourself in Icelandic culture, history, and nature. Try to learn a few phrases in Icelandic. The locals will appreciate your efforts, and it's a great way to connect with them.

And finally, when packing for your trip, remember that the weather in the Westfjords can be unpredictable. Warm layers, waterproof clothing, and good hiking shoes are essential. But, don't forget to leave a little room in your suitcase for the memories and stories that you'll inevitably collect during your time in the Westfjords.

To paraphrase J.R.R. Tolkien, you'll find that the road in the Westfjords often goes ever on and on, and that's the beauty of it. So, keep your eyes on the horizon, keep your spirit of adventure alive, and enjoy every moment of your journey in this extraordinary corner of Iceland. Safe travels, my friend, and enjoy the magical Westfjords.

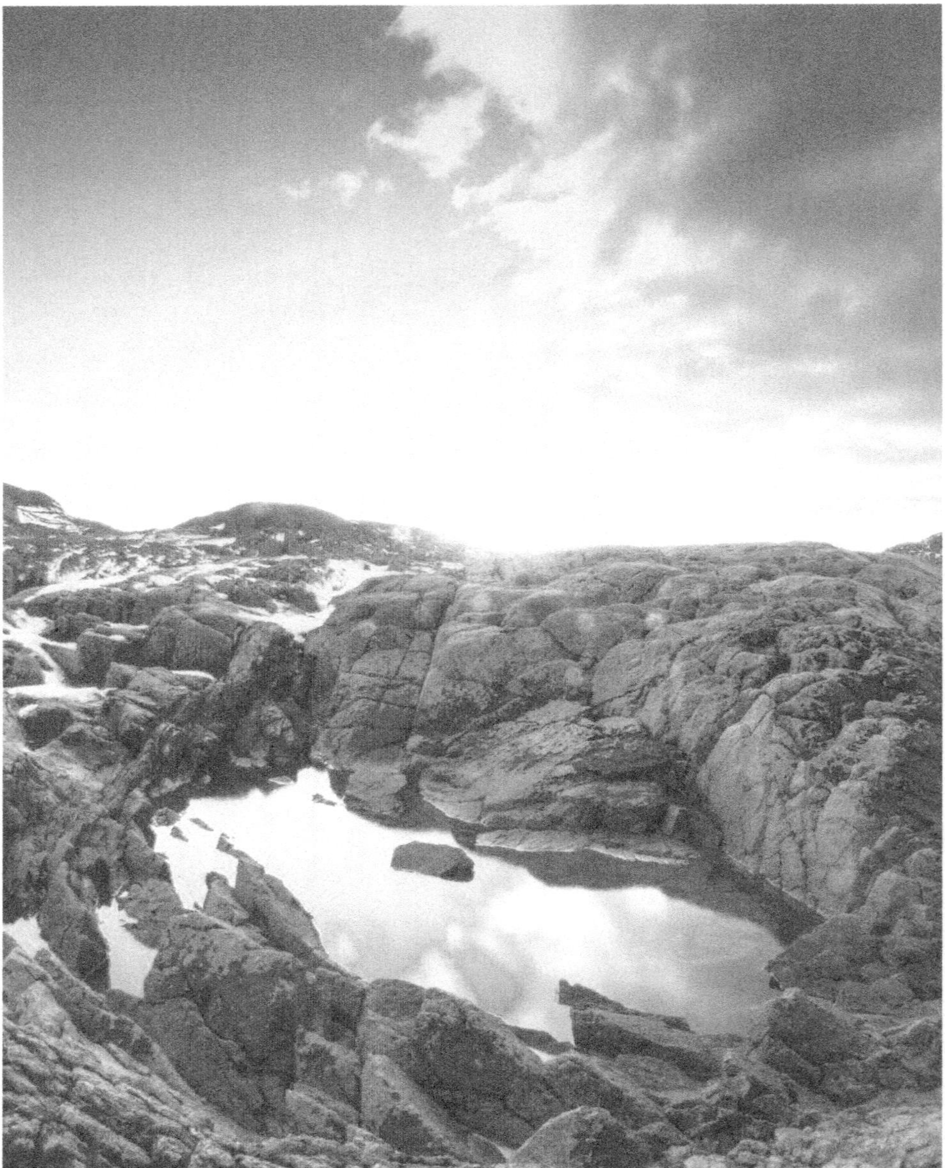

CHAPTER 5: EASTFJORDS

CHAPTER 5:
Eastfjords

Eastfjords, a little slice of Icelandic heaven, offers an unforgettable experience with its unique blend of natural beauty, local culture, and intriguing history. Like a rugged tapestry woven with towering mountains and deep fjords, it paints a mesmerising picture of seclusion and tranquility. This is a place where the wild meets the serene, and every curve of the road brings new landscapes waiting to be explored.

The region, defined by its spectacular fjords cutting into the highlands, provides ample opportunity for outdoor adventures, from hiking in verdant forests to spotting wildlife along the rugged coastline. But Eastfjords is not just about its great outdoors, it also hosts a collection of charming villages, each with its own personality and story, adding a dash of colour to the already impressive landscape.

Journeying through Eastfjords is like unearthing a treasure trove of Iceland's best-kept secrets. Off the beaten path, you will find a wealth of spots that seem untouched by time, adding an authentic dimension to your adventure. The remoteness only accentuates the sheer beauty of the region, inviting you to immerse yourself completely in the natural splendour that the Eastfjords have to offer.

In Eastfjords, the spirit of exploration is rewarded with awe-inspiring sights and experiences. Whether it's the enchanting Sey-

disfjordur, nestled between snow-capped mountains and cascading waterfalls, or the tranquil Borgarfjordur Eystri, famed for its puffin colonies, there's something to spark the wanderlust in every traveller. And if you're lucky, you might even spot the magical Northern Lights painting the night sky!
So, buckle up and get ready for a journey through the Eastfjords like no other, filled with remarkable discoveries and unforgettable memories. Keep reading to uncover the many surprises that this captivating region has in store for you. As your friend, I can assure you that your journey through Eastfjords will be one for the books!

Seydisfjordur

Seydisfjordur, a picturesque town tucked away in a deep fjord, is a hidden gem worth exploring in the Eastfjords. This idyllic location, adorned with pastel-coloured houses and surrounded by snow-dusted mountains, feels like a peaceful retreat from the world. One can't help but be enchanted by the town's magical landscape, where rainbows often arch across the sky after a soft drizzle.

The town is not just visually appealing; it's rich in history too. Seydisfjordur's roots date back to the early 19th century when Norwegian fishermen established a settlement here. Don't miss the Skaftfell Centre for Visual Art and the Technical Museum, which provides a glimpse into the town's fishing and industrial history. The iconic Blue Church, with its distinct blue exterior and white trim, also adds a unique charm to the town.
When visiting Seydisfjordur, consider timing your visit to coincide with the weekly Wednesday Market. This is when the town

truly comes alive, offering locally crafted products and food. The mid-summer LungA Art Festival is another notable event that transforms the town into a vibrant hub of creativity, attracting artists and spectators from around the world.

Borgarfjordur Eystri

Borgarfjordur Eystri, another quaint town in the Eastfjords, is a haven for wildlife enthusiasts and hiking lovers. Home to a large puffin colony, this area offers one of the best bird-watching spots in Iceland. From May to August, you can witness these adorable birds nesting in the cliffs around the harbour. For many travellers, watching puffins in their natural habitat is a highlight of their Iceland journey.

Apart from puffins, Borgarfjordur Eystri is also known for its superb hiking trails. The trails lead you through breathtaking landscapes, from lush valleys to majestic mountains. One of the most popular routes is the hike to Stórurð, a hidden oasis of turquoise ponds and giant boulders beneath the Dyrfjöll Mountains. It's a somewhat strenuous hike, but the spectacular views make it well worth the effort.

Pack a good pair of binoculars for bird-watching in Borgarfjordur Eystri, and remember to respect the wildlife by keeping a safe distance from the puffins and their nesting sites. If you're planning to hike to Stórurð, make sure to wear sturdy hiking boots, pack sufficient water and snacks, and check the weather conditions before you set off.

Papey Island

Off the coast of Eastfjords, you'll find Papey Island, a small, uninhabited island that serves as an exciting day-trip destination. The island, named after the Irish monks ('Papar') who are believed to have inhabited the island before the Viking Age, is rich in history and natural beauty.

Papey's biggest attractions are its large colonies of puffins and seals, making it an ideal spot for wildlife observation. The island's only building, a petite wooden church dating back to 1942, adds to its charm. From the top of the island, you're treated to panoramic views of the surrounding ocean and mainland.

Papey Island can only be reached by boat tours that operate from Djúpivogur during the summer months. These tours typically last around three hours and provide excellent opportunities for puffin watching and seal spotting. Remember to bring warm clothing as it can get chilly on the boat, even in summer.

Eastfjords Wildlife

The Eastfjords are a treasure trove of Icelandic wildlife. From puffins nesting on coastal cliffs to reindeer grazing in the highlands, animal lovers will find plenty to enjoy. The region is one of the few places in Iceland where you can spot wild reindeer, usually seen during the colder months when they descend from the mountains. Seals are often sighted lounging on the rocks or swimming in the fjords' calm waters.

Birdwatchers, too, are in for a treat. The Eastfjords are home to an array of bird species, including the colourful eider duck, white-tailed eagle, and numerous seabirds. The coastal cliffs teem with nesting birds in the summer, making it one of the best times to visit.

Make sure to respect the wildlife during your explorations. Maintain a safe distance and avoid causing any disturbances. This ensures the animals' safety and allows you to observe them in their natural state.

Hallormsstadur National Forest

Iceland may be known for its stark, treeless landscapes, but Hallormsstadur National Forest offers a refreshing change. Located near the town of Egilsstaðir, this forest is Iceland's largest, boasting a wide variety of tree species, including birch, aspen, and larch. The forest's tranquil atmosphere and beautiful scenery make it an ideal place for leisurely hikes and picnics.

Wandering through the forest, you'll find several marked hiking trails. One popular trail leads to the spectacular Hengifoss waterfall, the third highest in Iceland. The waterfall's striped cliff walls, a result of different volcanic eruptions, are truly a sight to behold.

While exploring Hallormsstadur, you might also come across the peaceful Lake Lagarfljót, where, according to local folklore, a mysterious serpent-like creature resides. Whether or not you spot the Lagarfljót Worm, the lake's shimmering waters and the surrounding scenery are sure to captivate you.

The Hidden Waterfalls of Eastfjords

While Iceland's major waterfalls like Gullfoss and Skógafoss draw the most attention, the Eastfjords host a number of hidden, lesser-known waterfalls that are equally stunning. A journey through the fjords reveals a landscape dotted with countless waterfalls cascading down rugged mountainsides, often with no one else in sight.

One such hidden gem is Folaldafoss, located on the old mountain road between Reydarfjördur and Egilsstaðir. This waterfall is particularly striking, with its pristine waters tumbling down into a beautiful blue pool.

A hike up the mountains often leads to more secluded waterfalls, providing an intimate experience with Iceland's nature. Just imagine the serenity of having these magical spots all to yourself. Just remember to tread lightly, respecting the environment to preserve these precious places for future visitors.

Eastfjords' Small Villages Exploration

The Eastfjords are dotted with charming small villages, each with its own unique character. While Seydisfjordur and Borgarfjordur Eystri might be the most famous, there are several other hidden gems worth exploring. These peaceful communities nestled between the sea and the mountains offer a glimpse into the authentic Icelandic way of life.

For instance, the quaint village of Stodvarfjordur is known for Petra's Stone Collection, an impressive private collection of rocks and minerals gathered from all over Iceland. Meanwhile, Fáskrúðsfjörður, historically a French fishing base, celebrates this heritage with a fascinating museum housed in former French buildings.

When visiting these villages, be sure to support the local economy. Whether it's buying a hand-knit sweater from a local artisan, savouring a meal at a family-run restaurant, or booking a room at a local guesthouse, your visit contributes to the sustainability of these small communities.

Eastfjords by Night

As night descends, the Eastfjords take on a different kind of beauty. Under clear skies, the fjords offer some of the best opportunities to view the Northern Lights in Iceland. The lack of light pollution in this rural area means the auroras are especially bright and visible.
On summer nights, instead of the Northern Lights, you'll experience the phenomenon of the Midnight Sun, when the sun barely dips below the horizon and the landscape is bathed in a beautiful, soft light. This time of year, the fjords' mountains and waters take on an ethereal quality that has to be seen to be believed.
Whether you're chasing the Northern Lights or basking in the glow of the Midnight Sun, the Eastfjords' night sky is sure to leave a lasting impression. Remember to pack warm clothes and a flask of hot chocolate to keep cozy as you enjoy the spectacle.

Day Trip to Storurd

If you're looking for an unforgettable hiking experience in the Eastfjords, consider a day trip to Storurd, one of Iceland's best-kept secrets. This remote area in the Dyrfjöll Mountains is home to a stunning mountain lake surrounded by enormous boulders and panoramic views of the fjords below.
Getting to Storurd requires a challenging but rewarding hike, best undertaken by experienced hikers. The trail can be hard to

find, so hiring a local guide is recommended. Despite the effort, the surreal beauty that awaits at the end is worth every step.

Once you reach Storurd, take some time to soak in the incredible surroundings. This is a perfect spot for a picnic, with the serene lake and towering peaks providing an unparalleled backdrop. Remember to leave no trace and help preserve this untouched piece of Icelandic wilderness.

Fjords Hiking

There's a profound sense of tranquility that accompanies hiking in the Eastfjords. This place is a dream for hikers, boasting various trails that wind through the region's fascinating landscapes. One moment you're navigating through vast fields of blooming lupine flowers, and the next, you're hiking up rugged mountains, gazing at the sweeping views below. The trails range from easy, relaxing strolls to more challenging treks that will push your limits, ensuring that every type of explorer will find their own adventure.

One of the must-see hikes in the Eastfjords is the trek to Hengifoss Waterfall, recognized as the third highest waterfall in Iceland. This beautiful natural wonder, set against a stunning backdrop of basalt columns and vibrant red clay layers, is truly a sight to behold. Imagine the soothing sound of rushing water echoing through the valley as you gaze at the majestic spectacle in awe.

If you decide to venture on this hike or any other, remember to check the weather conditions before you set out. Also, ensure that you have the necessary gear with you and inform someone about your hiking plans. Safety should always be your priority. Embrace the journey rather than focusing solely on the destination, and immerse yourself in the raw beauty that the Eastfjords hiking trails offer.

Eastfjords Cuisine

Delving into the culinary landscape of the Eastfjords is an adventure in itself. The region is renowned for its fresh, local produce, particularly the seafood. Imagine sitting in a cosy restaurant, the air filled with the delicious aroma of freshly caught langoustine or haddock, sizzling on the grill. Or perhaps you're in the mood for something truly Icelandic? In that case, hákarl, or fermented shark, could be a dish worth trying.

One eatery that stands out is Kaffi Kú, a charming café housed in an old cowshed in Borgarfjordur Eystri. Imagine settling down in this homely space, a steaming cup of coffee in hand, as you indulge in their delicious homemade cakes and sandwiches. As you gaze out of the window, you're greeted with a stunning view of the fjord, adding an extra layer of enjoyment to your meal.

But remember, it's not just about the food itself, it's about the whole experience. So take your time to savor each bite, chat with the locals, and soak in the ambiance. Whether it's a hearty meal after a long hike or a quick snack in between your explorations, the cuisine of the Eastfjords is sure to delight your taste buds and leave you longing for more.

Final Thoughts

To fully appreciate the magic of the Eastfjords, you need to take your time. This is not a region to be rushed. Embrace the slow pace, engage with the friendly locals, and let the natural beauty seep into your soul. There are still hidden gems waiting to be discovered, like the dramatic mountain landscapes of Neskaupstaður or the secluded beach at Breiðdalsvík.

One unique attraction that we haven't mentioned yet is the Wilderness Centre, an immersive museum located near Egilsstaðir. The Centre provides an intimate look at the history and lifestyle of the region's earliest settlers, offering a deeper understanding of Icelandic culture. You can even sleep in a traditional turf house for the full experience!

Remember, regardless of where your journey through the Eastfjords takes you, respect the fragile nature and wildlife that make this region so unique. The Eastfjords may be remote, but they offer a rewarding travel experience for those willing to venture off the beaten path. From breathtaking landscapes to rich cultural experiences, this enchanting corner of Iceland is sure to leave you with memories that will last a lifetime.

With that, I'll say cheers to your upcoming adventure in the Eastfjords. Enjoy every moment, and I hope this guide will make your journey even more fulfilling. Until next time, my friends, safe travels!

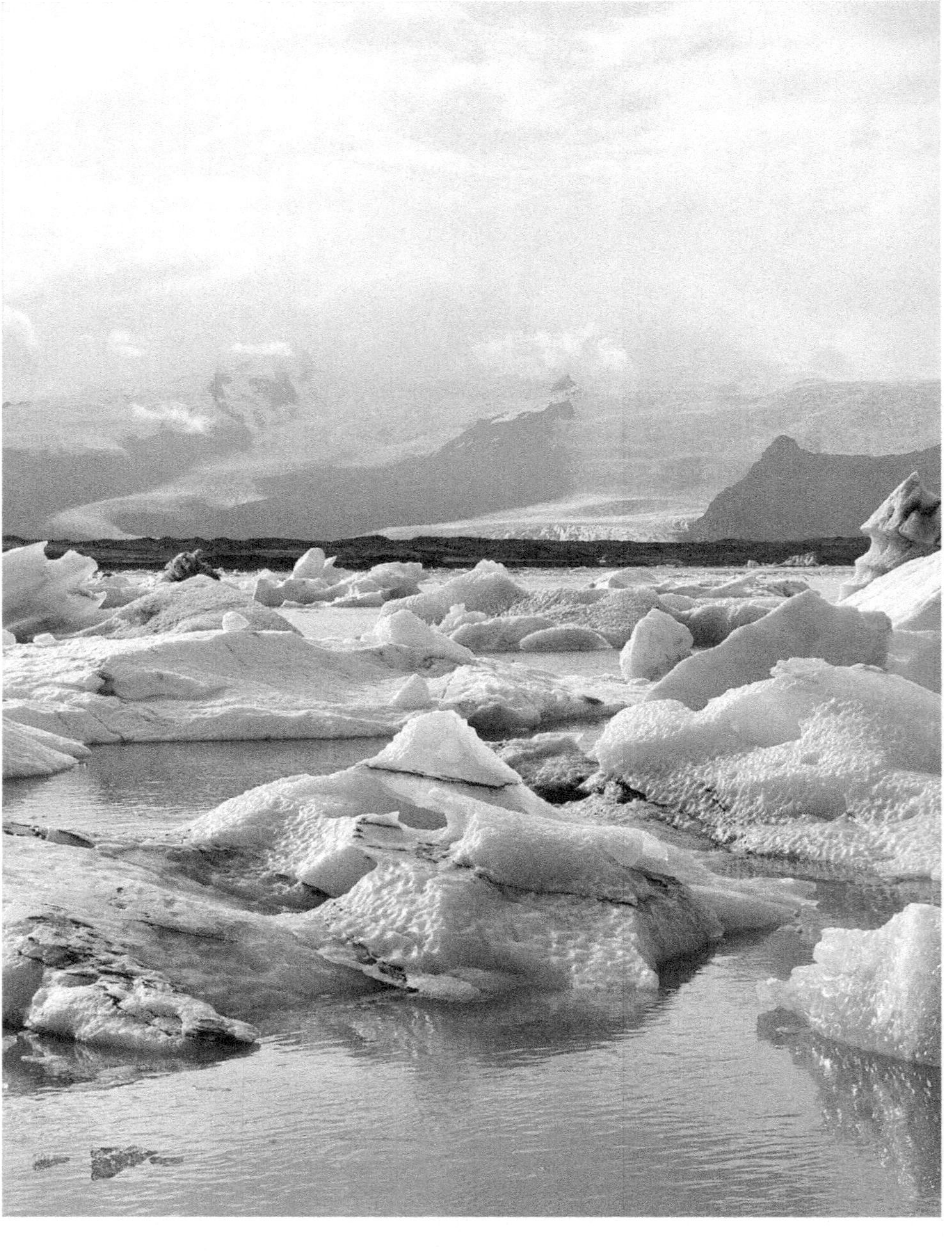

CHAPTER 6: NORTH ICELAND

CHAPTER 6:
North Iceland

North Iceland, a land of enchanting beauty, is bound to leave you utterly speechless. This region, with its towering waterfalls, hot geothermal springs, vast lava fields, and majestic glaciers, appears as though it's been plucked straight out of a fairy tale. Yet, it simultaneously exudes an aura of peace and serenity that feels almost tangible, making you feel like you've just stepped into another world entirely.

The bustling town of Akureyri, fondly known as the 'Capital of the North,' serves as a perfect gateway to the treasures of this region. Brimming with art and culture, it's a city you wouldn't want to bid farewell to anytime soon. With its charming old town, botanical gardens, and stunning views over the Eyjafjörður fjord, Akureyri sure knows how to make a lasting impression.

Lake Mývatn, famous for its geothermal activities, lava formations, and rich birdlife, is another must-visit on your North Iceland itinerary. One glimpse of its mystical landscapes, and you'll understand why it's been a setting for numerous films and television series.

And that's just the beginning. From the thrilling experience of whale watching in Húsavík to the awe-inspiring sight of waterfalls like Dettifoss and Goðafoss, the north will constantly keep you on your toes. If you're someone who appreciates the finer nuances of nature and enjoys venturing off the beaten track, you'll find North Iceland to be nothing short of a paradise.

So, fasten your seatbelts, my friend. This journey through North Iceland is going to be an adventure of a lifetime. Trust me; by the end of it, you'll have so many stories to share over a pint that your friends will be booking their tickets to Iceland right away!

Akureyri

Akureyri, often referred to as the 'Capital of the North,' is the perfect blend of culture, history, and natural beauty. It's the second-largest urban area in Iceland, bustling with activity and providing a plethora of experiences that cater to every type of traveler. Whether you're strolling through the enchanting old town, admiring the botanical gardens, or catching a performance at the theatre, there's something for everyone in Akureyri.

The Akureyri Church, with its distinctive architecture and impressive organ, is a definite must-see. The views of the town and the fjord from the top of the church steps are genuinely breathtaking. Then, there's the Akureyri Art Museum, showcasing contemporary works from Iceland and beyond.

Spend some time at the Listagil Art Street. It's a hub of creativity and culture, lined with galleries, studios, and boutique shops. Not to mention the eateries offering delicious local cuisine. It's the perfect place to soak up the city's vibrant atmosphere!

Lake Myvatn

Just an hour's drive east of Akureyri is the picturesque Lake Mývatn, a haven for nature enthusiasts and birdwatchers.

Formed by a massive volcanic eruption over 2000 years ago, the lake and its surroundings exhibit remarkable geothermal activity and unique lava formations.

One of the most popular attractions in the area is the Mývatn Nature Baths, a fantastic spot to relax and rejuvenate in geothermally heated waters with an awe-inspiring view. Don't forget to explore the Dimmuborgir lava field – home to the "Yule Lads," the 13 Icelandic versions of Santa Claus, according to local folklore.

Remember to pack your binoculars when visiting Lake Mývatn. It's a significant nesting site for various bird species, including ducks, making it a paradise for birdwatchers. Be prepared to spot some unique and rare species!

Husavik Whale Watching

If there's one thing you absolutely cannot miss while in North Iceland, it's the whale-watching tours in Húsavík. Often hailed as the whale watching capital of Europe, Húsavík offers you the chance to witness these majestic creatures in their natural habitat.

Most tours last for about 2-3 hours, during which you'll not only see various types of whales, including humpbacks, minke whales, and even blue whales but also seabirds like puffins. Moreover, the traditional Icelandic oak boats used for these tours add an authentic touch to the experience.

Make sure to visit the Húsavík Whale Museum. It provides a comprehensive insight into these fascinating marine mammals and their habitat. It's the perfect way to make the most of your whale watching experience in Húsavík.

Dettifoss Waterfall

Dettifoss, located in Vatnajökull National Park, holds the title of the most powerful waterfall in Europe, and witnessing its raw, untamed power firsthand is a spectacle you won't forget. The sheer force of the water crashing down is mesmerizing, creating a cloud of spray that adds an ethereal touch to the already stunning landscape.

You can view the waterfall from both the east and west banks. Each side offers a unique perspective, but remember, the west side has better facilities, including a car park and a visitor center, while the east side is more rugged and less developed.

Regardless of the side you choose, always ensure you have appropriate footwear. The area around the waterfall can be slippery, and a good pair of hiking boots will provide the necessary traction.

Also, always maintain a safe distance from the edge to prevent any accidents.

Godafoss Waterfall

Godafoss, or the 'Waterfall of the Gods', is another natural marvel that makes North Iceland so captivating. The waterfall gets its name from a historical event dating back to 1000 AD when Iceland officially converted to Christianity, and idols of the old Norse gods were thrown into the falls.

Godafoss might not be the biggest waterfall in Iceland, but its semi-circular shape and the resulting wide curtain of cascading water make it one of the most beautiful. The waterfall is easily accessible, with well-marked paths and viewing platforms that offer incredible views.

Visiting Godafoss during the winter provides an entirely different experience. The water takes on a turquoise hue against the snow-covered landscape, making for a spectacular sight. Do remember that the paths can be icy and slippery during this season, so extra caution is required.

The Arctic Henge

The Arctic Henge, located in the remote village of Raufarhöfn, is a monument to Norse mythology, serving as a tribute to the Eddic poem Völuspá. Consisting of a central column surrounded by a ring of smaller stones that align with the sun's path throughout the year, it mirrors the function of ancient stone henges in marking astronomical events.

Although still under construction, the Arctic Henge already provides a unique place for quiet contemplation amidst the wild Icelandic landscape. It's particularly magical during the midnight sun or the northern lights, when the play of light and shadows create an almost otherworldly atmosphere.

When planning a visit to the Arctic Henge, do take into account that it's in a remote part of North Iceland. Ensure that your vehicle is well-equipped for the road conditions, particularly during winter when the roads can be icy or snow-covered.

Lofthellir Ice Cave

One of the wonders of North Iceland is hidden beneath the surface, in the depths of the Lofthellir Ice Cave. Found in the volcanic Lake Mývatn region, the Lofthellir Ice Cave is a spectacular, 3500 years old subterranean world filled with magnificent ice sculptures and formations, illuminated by a soft, eerie glow. To get to Lofthellir, you'll embark on a somewhat challenging journey, including a 30-minute walk across a lava field, and the cave entrance is a small and narrow squeeze. But once inside, the sight of nature's icy artistry is truly worth it.

Visiting the Lofthellir Ice Cave is only possible with a guided tour and can be challenging due to icy, wet conditions. Dress warmly, wear waterproof clothing and sturdy shoes, and be prepared for a small but exciting adventure. Just don't forget to book your tour well in advance!

Tröllaskagi Peninsula

Jutting out into the Greenland Sea, the Tröllaskagi (Troll Peninsula) offers a rugged landscape of towering mountains, scenic fjords, and charming fishing villages. The peninsula is a fantastic spot for hiking and exploring the raw beauty of the Icelandic wilderness. It's also the perfect place to escape the more crowded tourist routes and experience an authentic slice of Iceland.

Hiking the trails that crisscross the peninsula is a great way to immerse yourself in the landscape. But for a unique experience, consider visiting the towns of Siglufjörður and Hofsós. Siglufjörður, once the center of Iceland's herring industry, houses the award-winning Herring Era Museum, while Hofsós offers one of the most picturesque swimming pools in the country.

Remember to pack good hiking shoes and rain gear, and always check the local weather forecast before setting out. A top tip is to try some of the locally caught seafood, renowned across Iceland for its freshness and flavor.

Ásbyrgi Canyon

Ásbyrgi Canyon is a spectacular geological formation located in the Vatnajökull National Park. According to Norse mythology, this horseshoe-shaped depression was formed by the hoofprint of Odin>s eight-legged horse, Sleipnir. Today, it provides one of the most enchanting hiking experiences in North Iceland.

Several trails weave through the canyon, ranging from easy to challenging. The Botnstjörn trail, which leads to a serene pond at the canyon's bottom, is a popular choice. For a panoramic view, take the trail leading to Eyjan ("the Island"), a rock formation in the middle of the canyon.

Hiking in Ásbyrgi is a joy in any season, but do remember to check the weather forecast and trail conditions before you set off. Equip yourself with sturdy shoes, warm clothing layers, and plenty of water. And don't forget your camera - you'll want to capture the canyon's ethereal beauty!

The Beer Spa

Imagine soaking in a warm tub filled with beer, water, hops, and yeast while sipping a local brew. Sounds dreamy, right? Bjórböðin, the beer spa located in Árskógssandur, offers exactly this unique relaxation experience. The treatment is said to have numerous health benefits, but most visitors come for the novelty and sheer enjoyment. Each tub is intended for one or two people, and there is no age limit for the bath because the bathwater is undrinkable. However, the beer tap at the side of the tub is only for guests over 20 years old.

Book your spot in advance as the spa has gained popularity among tourists and locals alike. Don't rush off after the soak;

spend some time in the relaxation room to let the brew's nutrients get absorbed into your skin. You'll leave feeling relaxed, rejuvenated, and with a fun story to tell!

North Iceland by Night

North Iceland unveils a different kind of magic as daylight gives way to darkness. One of the highlights is the chance to witness the spellbinding Northern Lights, or Aurora Borealis, paint the sky in vibrant hues of green, pink, and purple. This natural light display, caused by solar particles entering the Earth's atmosphere, is one of the most sought-after experiences in Iceland.

However, North Iceland by night isn't just about the Northern Lights. You can also explore the nightlife in Akureyri, where you'll find a range of cozy bars and clubs offering local craft beers and live music. Or simply enjoy the serene beauty of the landscape under the midnight sun during the summer months.

Remember that Northern Lights sightings are never guaranteed and depend on solar activity and clear skies. There are several apps and websites that provide forecasts to help you plan your aurora hunt. Dress warmly, and don't forget your camera and a tripod to capture this once-in-a-lifetime experience.

Day Trip to Grímsey Island

If you're looking to go off the beaten path, a day trip to Grímsey Island is a must. Located 40 kilometers off the north coast, Grímsey is the only place in Iceland that lies within the Arctic Circle. This tiny island, home to just a few dozen residents, is best known for its vibrant birdlife, including the adorable puffins that nest here in large numbers during the summer.

Getting to Grímsey involves a three-hour ferry ride from Dalvík or a short flight from Akureyri. Once there, you can walk around the entire island in a couple of hours, taking in the sight of cliffs teeming with seabirds, meeting friendly locals, and even standing with one foot in the Arctic Circle, marked by a striking monument called Orbis et Globus.

Bear in mind that weather conditions can change rapidly, so dress accordingly and make sure to check the ferry schedule in advance. If you're lucky, you might even spot whales during the ferry ride!

North Iceland Cuisine

The cuisine of North Iceland reflects the region's rich natural resources. You'll find dishes crafted from locally sourced ingredients like fresh fish from the surrounding seas, lamb from the lush pastures, and wild berries handpicked from the countryside. Akureyri, the 'Capital of the North', offers several top-notch restaurants where you can sample traditional dishes with a modern twist. Don't miss trying "plokkfiskur", a comforting fish stew, or enjoying a scoop of homemade ice cream from Brynja, a local favorite.

For foodies, a visit to the Myvatn region is a must, known for its "geysir bread", a rye bread baked underground by geothermal heat. And when in Husavik, don't miss the chance to taste the freshest seafood at one of the harborfront restaurants.

Remember, in Iceland, dining out can be quite expensive. So, it's worth looking out for lunch specials or sharing a few dishes between your travel companions to sample a wider range of Icelandic cuisine without breaking the bank. Bon appétit, or as the Icelanders say, "Verði þér að góðu"!

Final Thoughts

North Iceland truly is a treasure trove of natural wonders and hidden gems. Each town and fjord has its own unique charm and there are always more places to explore and experiences to enjoy. If you're looking for an offbeat adventure, try the charming island of Hrisey, often called 'The Pearl of Eyjafjordur'. A quick ferry ride from the mainland, Hrisey offers a sense of tranquillity you won't find elsewhere.

Driving in North Iceland is a dream, with well-maintained roads and awe-inspiring views at every turn. Just remember that the weather can be unpredictable, so always check conditions before setting off. An essential rule for exploring Iceland is to respect the nature - stick to marked paths and take only pictures, leave only footprints.

Make sure to try and time your visit to coincide with local events. The Great Fish Day in Dalvík is a highlight, where you can feast on free fish dishes cooked by the locals in August. Music lovers should not miss Akureyri's annual summer music festival, a haven for indie music lovers.

Don't be fooled into thinking North Iceland is only a summer destination. In winter, the region transforms into a snowy paradise, offering opportunities for skiing, ice fishing and the chance to witness the spectacular Northern Lights. In fact, Akureyri is considered one of the best places in Iceland to catch the aurora borealis.

In the end, the magic of North Iceland lies in its diversity - from bustling towns to serene landscapes, from midnight sun to mystical Northern Lights. It's a place that touches the soul, leaving you with memories that will last a lifetime. So here's to your journey in the North - may it be filled with awe-inspiring vistas, delicious bites, unexpected encounters, and a sense of peace that only the Icelandic nature can bring. Cheers, or as they say in Icelandic, "Skál"!

ICELAND TRAVEL GUIDE

CHAPTER 7: SNAEFELLSNES PENINSULA 99

CHAPTER 7:
Snaefellsnes Peninsula

Welcome to the Snaefellsnes Peninsula, often hailed as "Iceland in Miniature" due to the sheer diversity of natural wonders packed into this relatively small area. From soaring mountains to picturesque fishing villages, from volcanic craters to black sand beaches, Snaefellsnes has it all.

At the heart of the peninsula lies the magnificent Snaefellsjokull National Park, home to the famed glacier-capped volcano that served as the entrance to the center of the Earth in Jules Verne's classic novel. But that's just the beginning. With so many attractions dotted along its length, every turn on the peninsula's main road unveils a new spectacle.

It's not just about the nature either. The peninsula is dotted with charming small towns and fishing villages, where you'll find warm hospitality and delicious cuisine. Try the fresh seafood, indulge in traditional lamb soup, or explore the local breweries - each with their own unique take on Icelandic beer.

Despite its compact size, it's easy to spend several days exploring the Snaefellsnes Peninsula, each offering a different and exciting adventure. Whether you're taking a leisurely stroll along the rugged coast, exploring a centuries-old cave, or simply soaking in the breathtaking views from the comfort of your car, you're sure to be captivated by the magic of Snaefellsnes.

So, grab your camera, strap on your hiking boots, and let's set off to discover the wonders of the Snaefellsnes Peninsula. We have mountains to climb, waterfalls to admire, and delicious fish to eat. And who knows? If we're lucky, we might even spot a troll or two along the way. Let's go!

Snaefellsjokull National Park

Snaefellsjokull National Park is a testament to the raw, untamed beauty of Iceland. Dominating the landscape is the majestic Snaefellsjokull Glacier, an active stratovolcano topped by a glacier. Its impressive ice cap can be seen from Reykjavik on a clear day, standing as a beacon for adventurers and nature lovers. Here, you can hike to the top of the glacier in the summertime or explore the surrounding lava fields and caves that tell a millennia-old story of geological drama.

Numerous walking trails crisscross the park, leading you through lava fields and birch forests, past crater lakes and basalt cliffs. Take a walk along the Songhellir Cave, or "Singing Cave," so named for its unique acoustics, or explore the Rauðfeldsgjá Gorge, a deep, narrow fissure in the mountain's side. It's said that Bárður, a semi-mythical figure from the Icelandic sagas, threw his two nephews into this gorge!

The national park is also home to an incredible array of wildlife. Bird watchers will be in paradise here, with species such as puffins, guillemots, fulmars, and kittiwakes nesting in the cliffs. Just remember, leave only footprints and take only pictures. Our aim is to enjoy the beauty of the park and preserve it for future generations.

Kirkjufell Mountain

The distinctly shaped Kirkjufell Mountain is one of the most photographed landmarks in Iceland. This arrowhead-shaped peak stands alone on the edge of the sea, creating a striking backdrop to the nearby town of Grundarfjörður. With a waterfall conveniently located in the foreground, Kirkjufell offers the perfect composition for that postcard-perfect photograph.

If you're feeling energetic, the hike to the top of Kirkjufell is a rewarding challenge. The trail is steep and tricky in places, so be prepared. But the view from the top is absolutely worth it. You'll be rewarded with sweeping vistas of the peninsula and the sparkling sea beyond. However, always remember to respect the environment and stay on marked trails.

Visiting Kirkjufell in winter presents a different kind of spectacle. When the Northern Lights decide to put on a show, they dance over the mountain and reflect on the surrounding water bodies, creating a breathtaking scene straight out of a fairy tale. You'll need some luck to catch this natural phenomenon, but even without the auroras, Kirkjufell in the snow is a sight to behold.

Budir Black Church

Located in a stark landscape of black lava fields and yellow beaches, Búðir Black Church is an architectural gem. This tiny wooden church, painted entirely black, stands in contrast to the lush green moss and vibrant wildflowers that cover the surrounding lava field. It's a scene straight out of a fantasy novel.

The church dates back to the 19th century and is one of only a few black churches in Iceland. The color comes from the tar used to weatherproof the wood, a common practice in Scandinavian countries. Inside, it's a minimalist heaven, with a simple wooden pulpit and rows of pews.

There's something undeniably special about this place. Maybe it's the isolation, or the stark contrast of the black church against the surrounding landscape. Either way, it's a spot that begs you to sit, contemplate and enjoy the silence. Just a tip: the church looks even more mystical when shrouded in the mist, so if you wake up to a foggy day, you know where to head!

Fishing Villages of Snaefellsnes

The Snaefellsnes Peninsula, like much of Iceland, has a long history of fishing. Scattered along its coast are quaint little fishing villages, each with its own unique character and charm. These villages, with their colourful wooden houses and small harbors filled with fishing boats, are an integral part of the Icelandic way of life and a testament to the nation's hardy spirit.

One such village is Arnarstapi, which lies on the southern coast of the peninsula. It's a picture-perfect settlement, with beautiful cliffs nearby teeming with birds, and the iconic stone statue of Bárður Snaefellsás, a character from the Icelandic sagas. The village also serves as the starting point for a scenic coastal walk to Hellnar, another charming fishing hamlet.

Then there's Ólafsvík, the oldest trading town in the peninsula, known for its striking modern church and the nearby Ólafsvíkurfoss waterfall. And Grundarfjörður, home to the famous Kirkjufell Mountain, offers whale watching tours during summer months. When visiting these villages, don't forget to try the fresh seafood. After all, it doesn't get any fresher than this!

Djupalonssandur Beach

When you first set foot on Djúpalónssandur Beach, you might feel like you've landed on another planet. Located on the western coast of the Snaefellsnes Peninsula, Djúpalónssandur is a black pebble beach surrounded by tall, jagged lava rock formations. It's a wild and beautiful place, a stark reminder of the volcanic forces that have shaped Iceland.

One unique feature of this beach is the four large stones of different sizes, known as the lifting stones. These stones were used by fishermen in the olden days to test their strength. Each stone has a name corresponding to its weight, and if a fisherman could not lift the 'Hálfdrættingur', he was deemed unsuitable for a life at sea.

The beach is also home to the eerie remnants of a shipwreck - rusted pieces of metal scattered across the beach, slowly being reclaimed by nature. These remnants serve as a poignant reminder of the power of the sea. Always remember, while the beach is beautiful, the surf can be dangerous, so heed warning signs and keep a safe distance.

Gerðuberg Basalt Cliffs

Nestled in the middle of a moss-covered lava field, Gerðuberg Cliffs are a marvel of nature. These geometrically perfect basalt columns rise like a fortress wall, testament to the incredible geological forces at work in this land of fire and ice. They were formed by a volcanic eruption, where the lava cooled slowly and crystallized to form these striking hexagonal columns.

The cliffs are easily accessible by car, and there's a small parking area at the base. From there, you can walk right up to the cliffs for an up-close view of the basalt columns. Some of the columns are up to 14 meters high, and the cliff extends over 500 meters, making for a truly awe-inspiring sight.

While it's not permitted to climb on the cliffs, they make for some dramatic photographs, especially when the low sun casts long shadows over the basalt columns. This geological wonder is just another reason why the Snaefellsnes Peninsula is often referred to as 'Iceland in Miniature' - it's a small area, but it certainly packs a punch in terms of natural beauty.

Vatnshellir Cave

Beneath the lava fields of Snaefellsnes Peninsula lies Vatnshellir Cave, a hidden world of darkness and quietude. This 8,000-year-old lava tube was formed during a volcanic eruption and is now one of the most accessible and easily explored caves in Iceland. Guided tours will take you down a spiral staircase into the depths of the earth. Here, under the eerie glow of helmet lights, you'll discover peculiar rock formations, stalactites, and stalagmites. The colors and textures of the lava are truly a sight to behold, with the solidified lava walls sometimes appearing to shimmer with a silver glow.

One unique aspect of Vatnshellir is the utter silence that engulfs you as you descend deeper into the cave. All you can hear is the sound of your own breathing and the drip-drip of water echoing in the darkness. Remember to wear warm clothes, as temperatures inside the cave stay around 3-4°C throughout the year.

Snaefellsnes Peninsula by Night

When the sun sets, the Snaefellsnes Peninsula takes on a whole new dimension. With minimal light pollution, it becomes a stargazer's dream, the Milky Way stretching across the sky like a river of stars. But the real magic happens when the Northern Lights make their appearance, dancing and flickering across the night sky in shades of green, pink, and sometimes even red.

There's something truly mesmerizing about standing under the vast, dark sky, the iconic silhouette of Kirkjufell in the background, watching the aurora borealis perform its ethereal dance. It's a spectacle that never fails to take your breath away, no matter how many times you've seen it before. Make sure to check the aurora forecast before you go, and dress warmly - Icelandic nights can be chilly!

Day Trip to Stykkisholmur

Stykkishólmur, the largest town on the Snaefellsnes Peninsula, is well worth a day trip. This vibrant and charming harbor town is full of colorful, well-preserved houses from the Danish trading period, and is also famous for its seafood, particularly scallops and mussels.

One must-visit is the Volcano Museum, showcasing the art and culture associated with the volcanic landscape. Another iconic spot is the Stykkishólmskirkja, a modern white church offering panoramic views of the town and the sea. The harbor is also a bustling place with boats coming and going, and from here, you can take a boat tour to explore the nearby islands and birdlife. Don't miss a visit to Súgandisey Island Lighthouse, which provides a fantastic view of the town and the surrounding landscape. If you're a fan of Nordic Noir, you might recognize Stykkishólmur from the popular series "Trapped". Finally, before leaving town, try to catch a glimpse of the 'Búðakirkja', or the Black Church of Búðir, an iconic wooden church set in a lava field.

Snaefellsnes Road Trip

One of the best ways to explore the Snaefellsnes Peninsula is to embark on a road trip. From quaint fishing villages and black-pebble beaches to dramatic cliffs and waterfalls, this peninsula offers a wealth of diverse landscapes that are best explored at your own pace.

Begin your journey with a drive around the outer edges of the peninsula, where every turn in the road reveals another postcard-perfect view. As you make your way around, you'll pass through charming villages such as Arnarstapi and Hellnar, each one brimming with its own unique character and charm.

Make sure to allocate plenty of time for spontaneous stops and detours along the way. There's always a chance you'll come across a hidden gem off the beaten path. And don't forget to bring along a picnic, as there are plenty of scenic spots to pull over and enjoy a meal amidst the stunning landscape.

Snaefellsnes Cuisine

Snaefellsnes might be small, but when it comes to cuisine, it definitely punches above its weight. From fresh seafood caught in the nearby waters to locally sourced lamb and dairy products, the peninsula offers a delightful culinary journey.

One must-try dish is the local catch of the day, whether it's cod, haddock, or langoustine, grilled to perfection and served with locally grown vegetables. Another local favorite is 'Hangikjöt', smoked lamb, often enjoyed in a sandwich with Icelandic flatbread. And of course, no trip to Snaefellsnes would be complete without trying skyr, a traditional Icelandic dairy product similar to yogurt.

For those with a sweet tooth, the rhubarb cake is a delight, often made with rhubarb grown in local gardens. Paired with a cup of coffee, it's the perfect end to a day of exploring the peninsula's many attractions.

Final Thoughts

There's a certain magic about the Snaefellsnes Peninsula that you simply won't find anywhere else. Maybe it's the stark beauty of its landscape, the intriguing blend of the historical and the mystical, or the warm hospitality of the locals. Regardless of what draws you in, you're bound to leave with unforgettable memories and a desire to return.

Iceland is a place that encourages exploration and rewards curiosity. So, don't hesitate to venture off the beaten path, whether that's discovering a hidden beach, stopping by a local farm for fresh produce, or simply taking a moment to enjoy the view.

If you're visiting in winter, take the time to appreciate the austere beauty of the snow-covered landscape, and don't forget to look up at night for a chance to see the awe-inspiring northern lights. In summer, enjoy the long days and the midnight sun that lights up the sky even in the wee hours.

Snaefellsnes Peninsula, with its rich tapestry of natural wonders, is a microcosm of all that Iceland has to offer. And as you watch the sunset over the North Atlantic, Kirkjufell silhouetted against the sky, you'll understand why Iceland has a special place in the hearts of all who visit.

So, here's to your adventure on the Snaefellsnes Peninsula. May it be full of awe, wonder, and plenty of delicious Icelandic food. Skál!

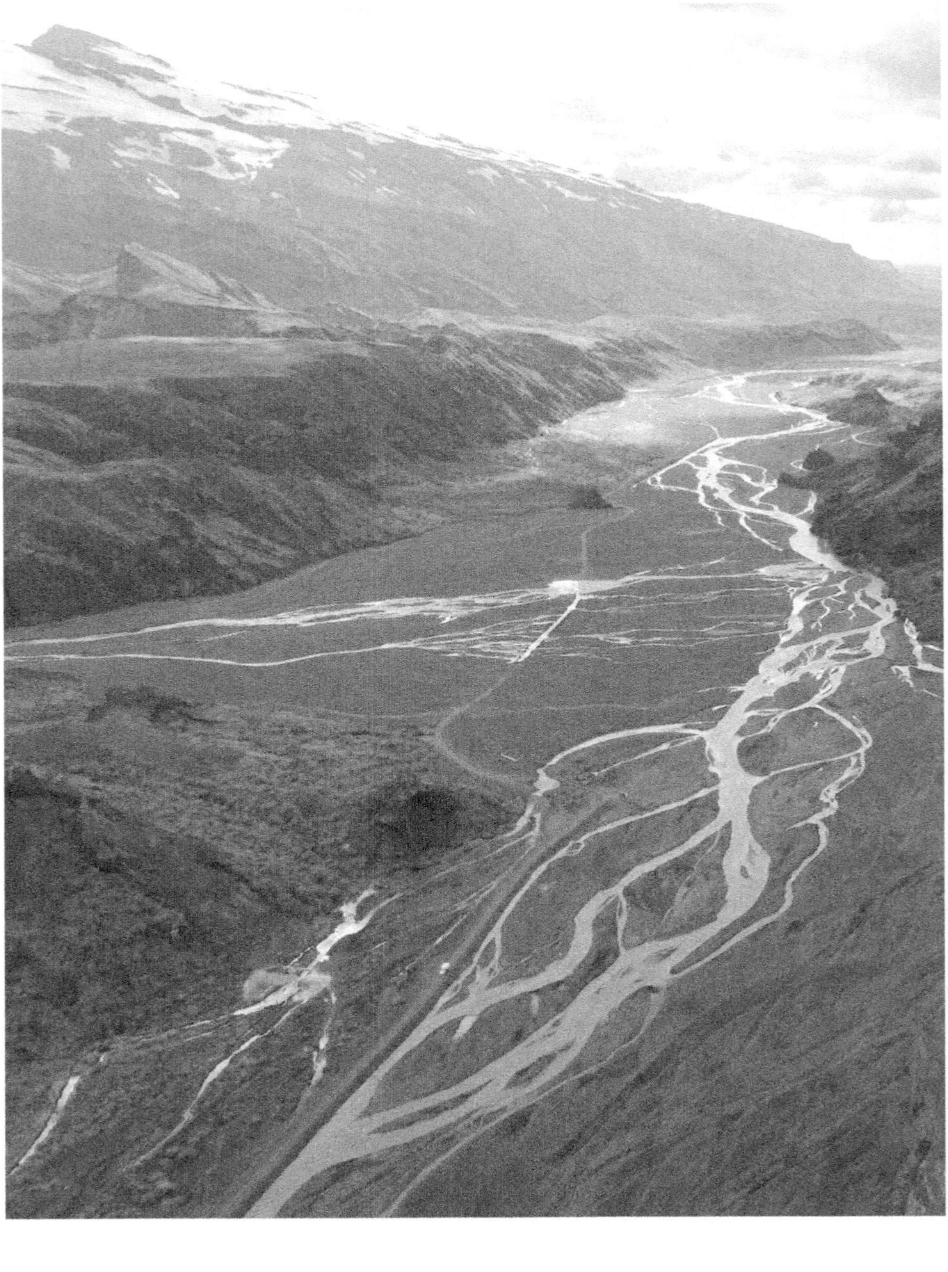

CHAPTER 8: HIGHLANDS 113

CHAPTER 8:
Highlands

Iceland's Highlands, often referred to as the "interior" of the country, are a vast expanse of untouched wilderness that holds some of Iceland's most spectacular natural wonders. This region is as rugged as it is breathtaking, a plateau of raw volcanic creation laced with rivers, and punctuated by mountains and glaciers. Its alien landscapes are the stuff of photographers' dreams and outdoor adventurers' thrills. Yet, despite the harsh environment, there's a profound silence and tranquility to this place, like it's Iceland's own secret sanctuary.

The Highlands are only accessible during the summer months, typically from late June until early September, when the mountain roads, known as F roads, open. The weather is harsh and unpredictable, making the region one of the most challenging, yet rewarding, parts of Iceland to explore. A four-wheel-drive vehicle is a must, and experienced driving skills are essential. The area is largely uninhabited, with only a few highland centers providing accommodation, food, and other services.

This vast, rugged region is home to some of Iceland's most stunning natural attractions, including Landmannalaugar, Askja, Thorsmork, Kerlingarfjoll, and many more. Hiking trails crisscross the area, leading you through a constantly changing panorama of lava fields, hot springs, geysers, waterfalls, and volcanic mountains. Whether you're looking to push your limits with challenging hikes, or simply bask in the awe-inspiring power of nature, the Highlands are a world waiting to be discovered. And when the day's adventure comes to a close, there's nothing quite like settling down under a sky full of stars, away from the city lights.

So, grab your hiking boots, pack your sense of adventure, and come prepared for a journey into the wild, into the raw heart of Iceland - its Highlands! Remember to respect the environment and leave no trace behind, ensuring these landscapes remain pristine for generations to come. Now, let's dive deeper into this untouched gem of Iceland!

Landmannalaugar

Located in the heart of the Icelandic Highlands, Landmannalaugar is renowned for its unearthly beauty. Imagine vast expanses of colorful rhyolite mountains, stretching to the horizon and beyond, interlaced with jet-black lava fields and interspersed with steaming hot springs. The vibrant colors of the hills range from pink to green, yellow, blue, purple, brown, black, and white. It's almost like stepping onto another planet, with landscapes so wild and wonderful, they defy description.

The area offers several hiking trails, the most popular of which is the Laugavegur Trail, considered one of the best hiking trails in the world. You'll also have the chance to relax in the natural geothermal pool after a day of hiking – an experience not to be missed. Don't forget to check out the Ljótipollur explosion crater, which despite its name meaning "ugly puddle", is incredibly beautiful with a turquoise-colored lake.

The best way to reach Landmannalaugar is by a 4x4 vehicle due to rough and often muddy roads. Alternatively, you can take a bus from Reykjavik during the summer months. Don't forget to pack warm clothing, even in summer, as the weather in the Highlands can be unpredictable.

Thorsmork

Thorsmork, or Þórsmörk in Icelandic, is a beautiful nature reserve nestled between three glaciers: Eyjafjallajökull, Mýrdalsjökull, and Tindfjallajökull. The area is named after Thor, the Norse god of thunder, and the epic landscapes certainly live up to the power and majesty of its namesake. A paradise for hikers, Thorsmork offers numerous trails leading through birch woods, along glacial rivers, and towards towering peaks.

There are several points of interest in Thorsmork, including the Krossá River, Valahnúkur hill, and the magnificent gorge of Stakkholtsgjá. For the intrepid, the 25-kilometer Fimmvörðuháls hike, starting in Skógar and ending in Thorsmork, provides a challenging but rewarding adventure.

Access to Thorsmork can be tricky due to the need to cross unbridged rivers. A 4x4 vehicle is a must. Alternatively, you can take a bus from Seljalandsfoss during the summer months. Always check the road conditions before setting out.

Askja

Located in the remote central highlands of Iceland, Askja is a massive volcanic caldera within the Dyngjufjöll mountains. It's most famous for its stunning lake, Öskjuvatn, and the smaller Víti crater filled with warm geothermal water where visitors can bathe. Askja's landscapes have a desolate, moon-like beauty, so much so that astronauts trained here for the Apollo missions.

The road to Askja is only accessible for a few months during the summer and requires a 4x4 vehicle due to river crossings and rough terrain. However, the trek is well worth it for the breathtaking vistas and the unique experience of swimming in a volcanic crater.

As with any trip in the Highlands, be prepared with warm clothing, good hiking shoes, and enough food and water. Always check the road and weather conditions before setting off. Guided tours are also available from Myvatn and Akureyri.

Rhyolite Mountains

There's an otherworldly beauty about the Rhyolite Mountains that you won't find anywhere else in the world. Known for their strikingly colorful landscapes, these mountains are a geological wonder, shaped by centuries of volcanic activity. The rhyolite stone gives the mountains their unique hues, which range from orange and pink to blue and green, depending on the light and weather conditions.

The most famous of these are in Landmannalaugar, an area known for its hiking trails and geothermal activity. The multi-colored hills, black lava fields, and steaming hot springs create an enchanting contrast that's a delight for the senses. It's like walking on an artist's palette, with each step revealing a new shade, a new landscape. Another site is Kerlingarfjöll, where the red rhyolite mountains contrast beautifully with the white snow and glaciers.

Exploring these mountains requires preparation. They are remote and often only accessible via rough mountain roads. As always, the weather can change rapidly, so it's crucial to check the forecast and road conditions before you head out. Respect the trails, take your trash with you, and don't forget to capture the enchanting beauty of these colourful landscapes!

Vatnajökull Glacier

Vatnajökull, the largest glacier in Europe, covers an astonishing 8% of Iceland's land area. It's a world of towering ice, with shimmering blue crevasses, imposing ice caves, and several active volcanoes hiding beneath its icy surface. The scale and majesty of Vatnajökull are awe-inspiring, serving as a poignant reminder of the forces that have shaped, and continue to shape, Iceland's landscape.

The glacier is home to several outlet glaciers, each with its unique charm and features. A popular one is Breiðamerkurjökull, which calves icebergs into the mesmerising Jökulsárlón Glacier Lagoon. Here, you can witness the power of the glacier as it carves the landscape, forming one of Iceland's most popular attractions.

Glacier tours, including hiking and ice caving, are popular ways to experience Vatnajökull, but safety is paramount. These tours should only be conducted with experienced guides and proper equipment.

Keep in mind that glaciers are living, moving entities, and conditions can change quickly. Your cooperation is essential in maintaining safety and ensuring that these majestic landscapes can be enjoyed by future generations.

Kerlingarfjoll Mountains

Nestled between the glaciers of Hofsjökull and Langjökull, in the heart of the Highlands, lies the mountain range of Kerlingarfjöll. It's a hiker's paradise with its well-marked trails, rhyolite mountains, geothermal valleys, and snow-capped peaks. This is a place where you can truly feel at one with nature, embracing the solitude and peace that comes with the remoteness of the area.

The crown jewel of the area is Hveradalir, a geothermal hotspot filled with steaming vents, bubbling mud pools, and brightly colored minerals. Hiking through this area feels like a journey to another planet. The contrast of the boiling earth and the icy peaks, the vivid colors and the barren landscape, it's a spectacle of Iceland's raw beauty.

The region is only accessible in summer, and it's crucial to have a 4x4 vehicle due to the challenging road conditions. If you plan to hike, make sure to have good hiking shoes and waterproof clothing, as weather conditions can change rapidly. And remember, stay on the marked trails to protect the fragile flora and ensure your safety. Kerlingarfjöll is an untouched piece of Icelandic wilderness, and it's our responsibility to keep it that way!

Hiking in the Highlands

Iceland's Highlands are the epitome of wild, unspoiled beauty, and there's no better way to explore them than on foot. The vast, untamed landscapes, characterized by rugged mountains, lava fields, and mossy plains, are a hiker's paradise. There's a thrill in immersing yourself in the raw and desolate nature, where every step leads to a new discovery.

Two of the most famous hiking trails in the Highlands are the Laugavegur Trail and the Fimmvörðuháls Pass. The former is a 55 km route from Landmannalaugar to Thorsmork, crossing multi-coloured rhyolite mountains, black sand deserts, and bubbling geothermal rivers. The latter is a stunning route that connects Thorsmork and Skogar, crossing between two glaciers and passing the Eyjafjallajökull volcano. The views are breathtaking, to say the least.

When hiking in the Highlands, it's crucial to be prepared. The weather can change quickly and dramatically, so layered clothing, rain gear, sturdy hiking boots, and ample food and water are a must. Always respect the environment, stick to marked trails, and inform someone about your hiking plans before you leave. Remember, safety is your responsibility, but the reward is an unforgettable adventure in some of the most stunning landscapes you'll ever see.

Highlands by Night

There's a certain magic to the Icelandic Highlands by night. As the light fades and the vast landscapes merge into silhouettes, a profound sense of calm sets in. If you're camping in the Highlands, the experience can be even more rewarding. Imagine falling asleep under a sky full of stars, with the sounds of nature as your lullaby. And if you're lucky, the Northern Lights might put on a show that you'll never forget.

Camping is allowed in designated campsites, and it's a popular choice among hikers and nature lovers. Campsites like Landmannalaugar, Thorsmork, and Kerlingarfjoll offer facilities such as toilets, showers, and sometimes even a warm pool to soak in after a long day of hiking.

However, camping in the Highlands requires some preparation. It can get chilly at night, even in summer, so make sure to bring a good sleeping bag, warm clothes, and food supplies. Also, be aware that wild camping is strictly forbidden in Iceland. Always respect the rules and the environment, leaving the place as you found it. The night in the Highlands is a unique experience that will make your Iceland adventure even more special.

Day Trip to Hveravellir

If you're looking for an escape from the beaten path, a day trip to Hveravellir Nature Reserve is just what you need. Nestled between two glaciers, Langjökull and Hofsjökull, Hveravellir is one of Iceland's most spectacular geothermal areas. It's a place where the earth is boiling, steam is rising, and the ground is painted in vibrant hues of green, yellow, and red.

At Hveravellir, you can explore hot springs, boiling mud pools, and a geothermal heated pool where you can take a dip surrounded by the Icelandic wilderness. The nature reserve also offers several hiking trails, where you can witness the power of the earth up close.

The road to Hveravellir is rough, and a 4x4 vehicle is recommended. Make sure to check road and weather conditions before you head out. And, as always, respect the environment, stay on marked trails, and leave no trace behind. A day trip to Hveravellir is an adventure into the heart of Iceland's geothermal activity, offering a unique and memorable experience.

Laugavegur Trail

Often considered the best long-distance trail in Iceland, the Laugavegur Trail is a magnificent, 55-kilometer trek that winds through some of the most diverse and spectacular landscapes in the Highlands. Starting from the geothermal wonderland of Landmannalaugar and ending in the verdant valley of Thorsmork, the trail will lead you across rhyolite mountains, geothermal valleys, glacial rivers, and lush moss-covered lava fields. It's no wonder that this trail is on the bucket list of every avid hiker.

The trail can be completed in 3 to 5 days, depending on your pace and how much you want to soak in the beauty around you. There are several huts along the way where you can rest, recharge, and share stories with fellow hikers. But remember, booking these huts well in advance is essential as they fill up quickly during the summer.

Trekking the Laugavegur Trail is a journey like no other. It's challenging, yes, but the feeling of accomplishment, the camaraderie on the trail, and the awe-inspiring beauty around every corner make every step worth it. Just remember to pack smart, respect the trail, and leave no trace behind.

Highlands Cuisine

Eating in the Highlands can be an adventure in itself. Since you're far from the hustle and bustle of cities and towns, you'll likely be cooking your meals. There's something profoundly satisfying about preparing a warm, hearty meal after a long day of hiking, especially if you can share it with new friends at a mountain hut or a campsite.

If you're trekking for multiple days, lightweight, high-energy foods like pasta, rice, dried fruits, nuts, and energy bars are recommended. And don't forget a hot beverage to keep you warm and hydrated! Packing a portable stove is a good idea, and remember to clean up after yourself and leave no trace.

However, don't let the remote location fool you into thinking you won't find gourmet food in the Highlands. If you happen to visit the Highland Center Hrauneyjar, you'll be pleasantly surprised by their restaurant, which serves delicious Icelandic lamb and fresh fish, along with vegetarian and gluten-free options. Trust me, it's an unexpected culinary delight in the heart of the wilderness.

Final Thoughts

And so, we've reached the end of our Highlands adventure. It's hard to put into words the raw, untamed beauty of this part of Iceland. The Highlands are a place where you can truly connect with nature, test your limits, and discover landscapes that seem out of this world.

That said, the Highlands are not a place to be underestimated. It's an area where you need to be well-prepared and aware of your surroundings. The weather can change quickly, the roads can be rough, and amenities are sparse. It's crucial to have a sturdy 4x4 vehicle, especially if you plan to visit places like Askja or Hveravellir. And always check road and weather conditions before you head out.

However, the effort is well worth it. Whether it's the multi-coloured mountains of Landmannalaugar, the dramatic landscapes of Thorsmork, the geological wonders of Askja, or the enchanting beauty of the Kerlingarfjoll Mountains, the Highlands are filled with wonders that will etch themselves into your memory.

Remember, when it comes to exploring the Highlands, it's all about the journey, not just the destination. So take your time, soak in the landscapes, respect the environment, and embrace the adventure. After all, as they say in Iceland, 'Glacier walks may be cold, but they're never boring'.

Oh, and before I forget, if you're visiting in the summer, try to squeeze in a visit to Sigöldugljúfur. It's a hidden gem not far from Landmannalaugar, a beautiful canyon filled with countless waterfalls. It's not as famous as some other spots in the Highlands, but trust me, it's worth the detour. Just another tip from a friend who has been there and been amazed.

Here's to your adventure in the Icelandic Highlands, my friend. Safe travels, and may the road lead you to unforgettable experiences. Skál!

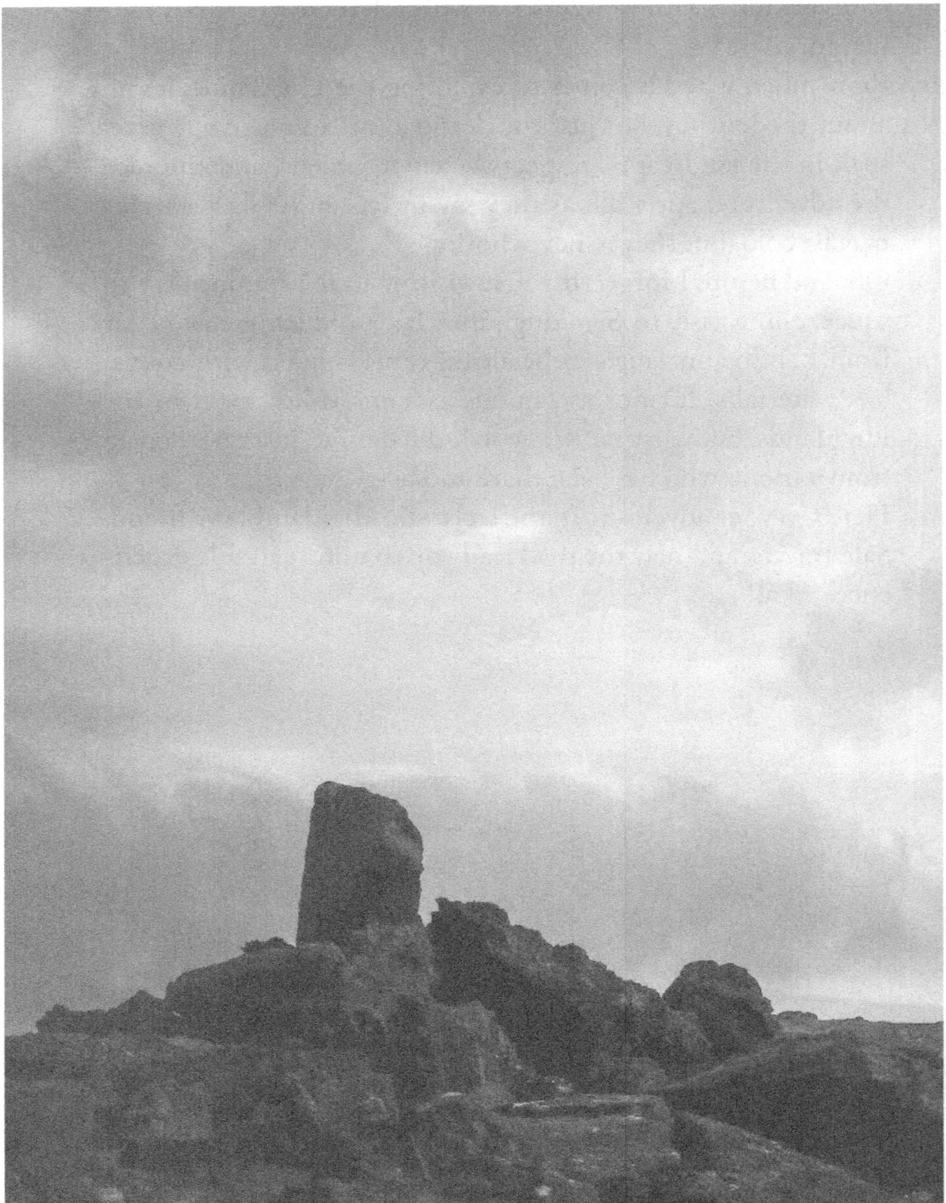

CHAPTER 9: REYKJANES PENINSULA   127

CHAPTER 9:
Reykjanes Peninsula

Welcome to the Reykjanes Peninsula, a region of stark beauty and dramatic landscapes, where the forces of nature take center stage. The peninsula, located in the southwest of Iceland, is often the first taste of the country for many visitors, given its proximity to Keflavik International Airport. But don't be mistaken - Reykjanes isn't just an entry point to Iceland, it's a destination in its own right.

In this part of the country, the earth feels alive. It's a land where geothermal activity bubbles beneath your feet, where volcanic craters and lava fields stretch as far as the eye can see, and where the rugged Atlantic coastline relentlessly pounds against black-sand beaches and towering cliffs. Yet, amidst all this raw natural power, there's a sense of tranquility and solitude that's almost surreal.

Reykjanes is home to some iconic Icelandic sights, like the world-famous Blue Lagoon and the Bridge Between Continents. But it also houses some less-known treasures like the geothermal area of Gunnuhver, the eerie Reykjanes Lighthouse, and the vibrant geothermal area of Krysuvik-Seltun. There's also a rich Viking history to explore and delicious local cuisine to savor.

Whether you're soaking in the warm, mineral-rich waters of the Blue Lagoon, feeling the heat from geothermal steam vents, or standing on a bridge that straddles two tectonic plates, Reykjanes offers an unforgettable introduction to the power and beauty of Iceland's nature.

We're here to guide you through the best that Reykjanes has to offer, with some insider tips and suggestions along the way. So grab your adventurous spirit, and let's embark on this journey together. Here's to exploring the mystical landscapes of Reykjanes!

Blue Lagoon

The Blue Lagoon is perhaps the most iconic sight in the Reykjanes Peninsula and one of the top attractions in Iceland. Set amidst a stunning lunar-like landscape, the geothermal spa's milky blue waters are rich in minerals like silica and sulfur, reputed for their skin-healing properties. The warm waters, steamy atmosphere, and surrounding black lava rocks create a surreal and relaxing experience you won't easily forget.

The lagoon's facilities are top-notch, with options ranging from standard entrance to more luxurious packages. And while you're floating in the warm waters, why not try a silica mud mask? It's included in your entrance and leaves your skin feeling incredibly soft and rejuvenated.

As the Blue Lagoon is one of Iceland's most popular spots, it's worth booking your visit in advance to ensure you get a spot. Try to go early in the morning or later in the evening to avoid the busiest times and make the most of this unique experience.

Gunnuhver Geothermal Area

Gunnuhver is a wildly active geothermal area named after an angry female ghost, Gudrun, whose spirit was trapped in the hot springs by a priest hundreds of years ago. The area is dotted with steaming vents and boiling mud pools, with the largest mud pool being around 20 meters wide. The colorful mineral deposits surrounding the springs create a surreal and otherworldly scene.

The wooden walkways provide safe and easy access around the geothermal area, so you can get up close and personal with this incredible demonstration of Earth's power without disturbing the delicate ecosystem. And as you explore, don't forget to listen; the sounds of the hissing steam and bubbling mud add an extra dimension to your visit.

To make your visit to Gunnuhver even more memorable, be sure to bring a camera. The contrasting colors and geothermal activity make for fantastic photography, especially if you're lucky enough to visit on a clear day.

Bridge Between Continents

The Bridge Between Continents, or Miðlína, is a small footbridge over a major fissure which provides clear evidence of the tectonic plate movements that have shaped Iceland over the centuries. The bridge was built as a symbol of connection between cultures and is a place where you can stand with one foot in North America and the other in Europe.

The bridge isn't big or grand, but it's the significance of the location that makes it special. It's a tangible sign of the geological forces that shape our planet, and there's something humbling about standing on a fault line, seeing the Earth's crust pulled apart by natural forces.

While it's certainly a unique photo opportunity, remember to take a moment to appreciate the magnitude of the geological forces at play. After all, how often can you say you've straddled two continents in one day?

Reykjanes Lighthouse

Perched on the southwestern tip of the Reykjanes Peninsula, Reykjanes Lighthouse is a beacon of solitude amidst the rugged coastline. The current lighthouse, built in 1907, is the oldest of its kind in Iceland, standing proud against the backdrop of crashing waves and black lava fields. It's not just a picturesque spot but also a monument to Iceland's maritime history and the critical role that lighthouses have played in ensuring sailors' safety.

Nearby, the impressive Gunnuhver geothermal area adds to the locale's appeal, and the surrounding cliffs serve as a haven for numerous seabird species, including puffins during the summer months. Pack a picnic and take in the serene views, listen to the symphony of bird calls and the distant lull of the ocean.

Don't forget to check out the nearby Reykjanes Art Museum, which often features work by local artists. The contrast of the wild, natural beauty of the area and the vibrant, human-made art pieces make for a particularly memorable experience.

Krysuvik-Seltun

Krysuvik-Seltun is a striking geothermal area located in the middle of the Reykjanes Peninsula. The bubbling mud pools and hissing fumaroles create an otherworldly atmosphere, further heightened by the pungent smell of sulfur that hangs in the air. Wooden boardwalks wind through the colorful landscape, allowing you to safely explore the area and get a closer look at the geothermal activity.

Aside from the geothermal area, Krysuvik-Seltun is also known for its hiking trails. One of the most popular paths leads to the top of Sveifluhals, a mountain offering panoramic views over the bright green Lake Grænavatn and the surrounding landscape.

For an immersive experience, visit during autumn or winter when the ground is a patchwork of red, orange, and yellow. The vivid hues of the landscape, combined with the blue of the geothermal pools, create a vibrant contrast that's a feast for the eyes.

Volcanic Fissures

The Reykjanes Peninsula, part of the Mid-Atlantic Ridge, is home to numerous volcanic fissures - visible scars left by magma forcing its way to the surface. Walking alongside these fissures, one can't help but feel a sense of awe at the raw power that has shaped, and continues to shape, Iceland's landscape.

The most famous of these is the Eldvörp cave row, a ten-kilometer-long crater row filled with a series of gaping fissures and steam vents. It's an excellent place to truly appreciate the peninsula's volcanic nature. The lava field here, known as Svartsengi, is dark and twisted, with moss adding splashes of green to the blackened landscape.

Remember to stay safe while exploring. Keep to marked paths and avoid getting too close to the edges of fissures. It's also worth noting that weather in the area can change quickly, so it's essential to dress in layers and bring waterproof gear. Despite the stark landscape, the region has an ethereal beauty that makes it well worth exploring.

Viking World Museum

The Viking World Museum, located in Njardvik, is a must-visit for anyone interested in Icelandic history and culture. The museum's star attraction is the Íslendingur (the Icelander), a painstakingly accurate replica of the famous Gokstad ship discovered in Norway. This authentic representation of a ninth-century Viking ship, which sailed to New York in 2000 to commemorate Leifur Eiríksson's journey to the New World, offers a tangible link to the past, a testament to the navigational skills and craftsmanship of the Vikings. In addition to the ship, the museum boasts five exhibitions that delve into different aspects of Viking culture, including their mythology, daily life, and their exploration of North America. There's also a charming café, with beautiful views over the ocean, where you can sit down for a steaming cup of coffee and a traditional Icelandic pastry.

A visit to the Viking World Museum offers a well-rounded, informative experience. It's not just about the historical aspect; it's also a chance to better understand the spirit of exploration and adventure that's deeply rooted in Icelandic culture. This is a place that encourages you to imagine, to connect with a time long gone but not forgotten.

Reykjanes Peninsula by Night

Experiencing the Reykjanes Peninsula by night offers a whole new perspective on this remarkable region. As the day fades and twilight sets in, the peninsula's features take on an ethereal quality, with the moonlight reflecting off the black lava fields and the Atlantic Ocean's waves gently crashing against the shoreline. This, however, is just a precursor to the real spectacle - the Northern Lights.

When conditions are right, the Reykjanes Peninsula is an excellent spot for Northern Lights hunting. The limited light pollution and expansive landscapes make for perfect viewing conditions. Watching the auroras dance and ripple across the night sky, their colors casting an otherworldly glow over the rugged landscape, is a sight that leaves even the most seasoned travelers awestruck.

Remember, spotting the Northern Lights is never guaranteed, and depends on solar activity and weather conditions. Nonetheless, standing under the vast, star-studded sky of the Reykjanes Peninsula, you'll feel a deep connection to the cosmos, whether the elusive lights decide to make an appearance or not.

Day Trip to Grindavik

Grindavik, a charming fishing village on the Reykjanes Peninsula's southern coast, makes for an excellent day trip. Its picturesque harbor, populated by colorful fishing boats, and surrounding lava fields provide an insight into traditional Icelandic coastal life. The town itself, though small, is vibrant and welcoming, with well-preserved houses, local arts and crafts shops, and the indispensable fish and chips stand serving up freshly caught seafood.

One of the main draws of Grindavik is its proximity to the Blue Lagoon, but there's much more to it. The Grindavik swimming pool, for instance, is a lesser-known gem that offers geothermal hot tubs, a steam bath, and a waterslide. After a day of exploring, soaking in these hot tubs is the perfect way to relax and soak up the local culture.

Remember to pay a visit to the Saltfisksetrid Museum, where you can learn about the significant role that the fishing industry played in Iceland's development. The museum provides a detailed and engaging history of the industry, and even offers samples of the traditional dried fish snack, hardfiskur. Grindavik's charm lies in its simplicity and authenticity, offering visitors a unique glimpse into the Icelandic way of life.

Exploring Reykjanes by Car

Hitting the road and exploring the Reykjanes Peninsula by car is an adventure you won't want to miss. The peninsula's compact size and well-maintained roads make it an ideal region for a self-drive tour. From the lunar-like landscapes of the Leif the Lucky Bridge to the serene seaside vistas around Grindavik, every turn reveals a new, captivating sight.

A highlight of any self-drive itinerary has to be the Reykjanesviti, Iceland's oldest lighthouse. Positioned on a cliff edge overlooking the wild Atlantic, its setting is as dramatic as it is beautiful. Another stop that should definitely be on your list is Seltún geothermal area, where you can stroll on wooden pathways amidst bubbling mud pools and steam vents.

When you have your own set of wheels, you have the freedom to explore at your own pace. You can stop to take in the stunning views, enjoy a picnic lunch by a secluded cove, or simply pull over to capture that perfect photo. Remember, the best part about road trips is the journey, not just the destination. Don't rush it—embrace the spirit of the Icelandic "þetta reddast" (everything will work out) and see where the road takes you.

Reykjanes Cuisine

The cuisine of the Reykjanes Peninsula mirrors the region's coastal surroundings, with fresh seafood being a staple in the local diet. The fishing towns dotted around the peninsula provide an array of delightful dining options, where you can savor dishes made from the day's catch. Whether it's succulent lobster soup in Grindavik or salted cod in Keflavik, the taste of the ocean is unmistakable.

Icelandic lamb is also not to be missed. Raised free-range during the summer months, the lamb in Iceland has a distinct, delicate flavor that's worth trying. A visit to a local farm or a restaurant serving farm-to-table fare is the best way to enjoy this Icelandic specialty.

And then, there's the dairy. Icelandic skyr, a thick, yogurt-like dairy product, is something you'll find in every local's fridge. Enjoy it with fresh berries for breakfast, or try it in a smoothie for a healthy snack. As always, the joy of food lies in trying new things, so don't be afraid to step out of your comfort zone when dining on the peninsula.

Final Thoughts

The Reykjanes Peninsula, with its rugged landscapes and rich cultural heritage, is a microcosm of all that Iceland has to offer. It's a place where geothermal energy bubbles just beneath the surface, where the Northern Lights dance across the night sky, and where the harshness of the volcanic landscape is softened by the warmth and resilience of the Icelandic spirit.

A trip to the Reykjanes Peninsula is a journey into the heart of Iceland's geological and cultural marvels. But it's more than just a collection of tourist attractions - it's a place that invites you to pause, to look closer, and to connect with the raw, wild beauty of the land. The peninsula's charm lies not only in its spectacular sights, but also in its quieter moments: the gentle rustle of wind over lava fields, the soothing melody of ocean waves, the welcoming smile of a local.

As you plan your trip, don't forget to leave some time for the unexpected. Maybe you'll stumble upon a small, secluded beach, or find a hiking trail that leads you to stunning views. Perhaps you'll discover a local restaurant serving the best fish and chips you've ever tasted, or find yourself gazing at a sunset that sets the sky ablaze with color.

Exploring the Reykjanes Peninsula isn't about ticking off a checklist of sights; it's about immersing yourself in the experience, the adventure, the wonder. Whether you're soaking in the Blue Lagoon, trekking across a moss-covered lava field, or simply enjoying the peace and solitude of a midnight stroll, the Reykjanes Peninsula is a place that stays with you long after you've left.

So pack your bags, set your GPS, and get ready to uncover the magic of the Reykjanes Peninsula. We guarantee it will be an adventure you won't soon forget.

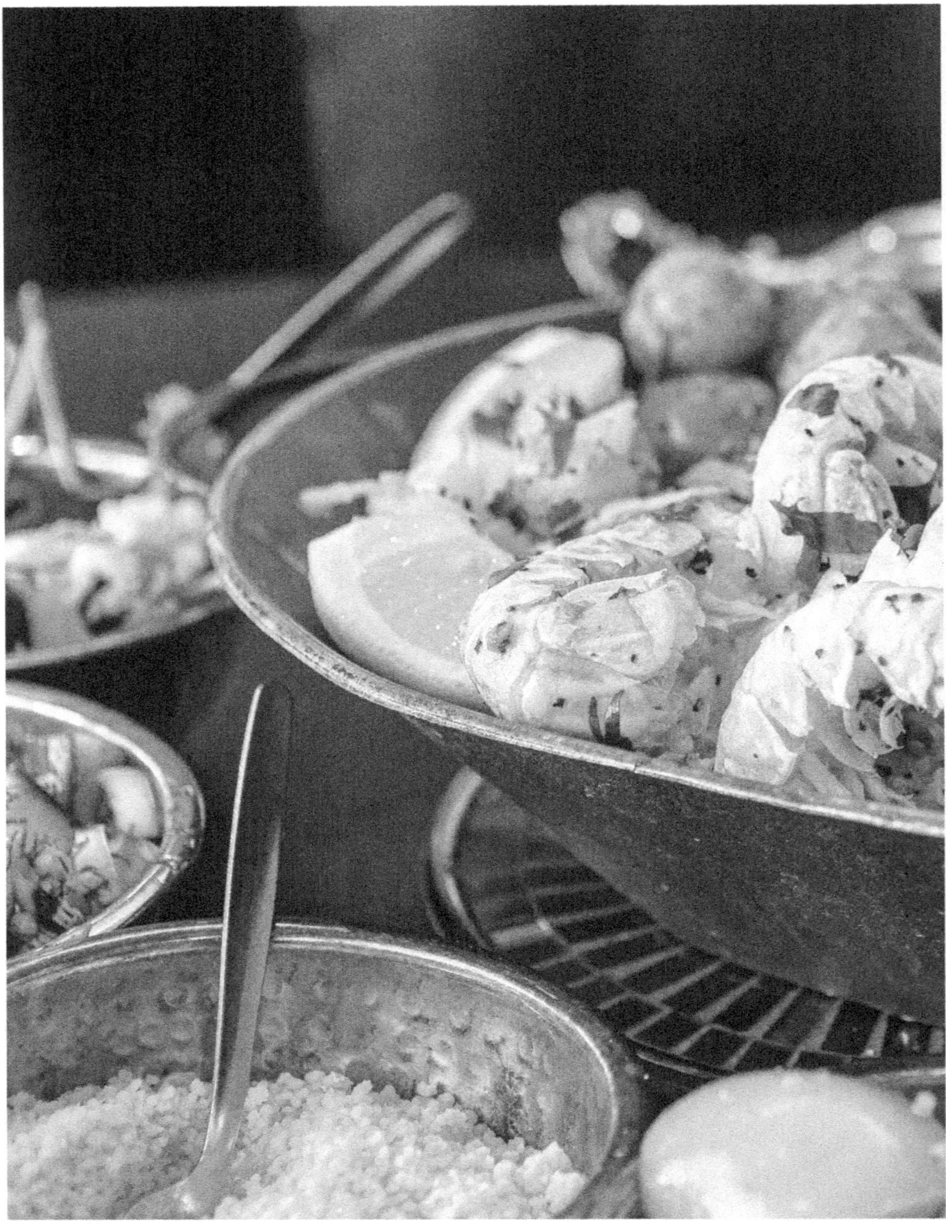

CHAPTER 10: ICELANDIC CUISINE

CHAPTER 10:
Icelandic Cuisine

Delving into Icelandic cuisine is like taking a sensory journey through the country's cultural history and diverse landscapes. Rooted in the harsh climate and isolated location, the traditional food of Iceland is a testament to human resilience, ingenuity, and the bounty of nature. Today, this rugged Nordic nation serves up a gastronomic scene as impressive as its volcanic landscapes, northern lights, and gushing geysers.

As you travel through Iceland, you'll discover a cuisine that reflects the surrounding landscapes: from the freshest fish and seafood harvested from the icy North Atlantic and Arctic waters, to lamb raised on lush, verdant pastures during the summer months. It's food that tells a story of its place of origin, that connects you with the land, the sea, and the people who live there.

Icelandic cuisine can be wonderfully surprising for first-time visitors. It's about more than just fuelling your body; it's about experiencing the culture, the traditions, and the very spirit of Iceland. Every meal is a new adventure, whether you're sampling home-baked rye bread cooked in a geothermal hot spring, trying 'hot spring' eggs boiled in geothermal waters, or daring to taste the infamous fermented shark.

From savoring traditional dishes that have sustained Icelanders for centuries to indulging in innovative dishes from award-winning restaurants, exploring the Icelandic food scene is sure to be a highlight of your trip. In this chapter, we'll take a closer look at some of the country's iconic dishes, food festivals, regional specialties, and even vegan and vegetarian options.

So, loosen your belt and prepare your taste buds for a culinary journey like no other. Velkominn to Icelandic cuisine – the wild, the fresh, and the downright delicious.

Skyr

Skyr is more than just a yogurt-like dairy product; it's an essential part of Icelandic culture. Dating back over a thousand years to the Viking era, Skyr's mild flavor and creamy texture make it a staple on every Icelandic table. You can have it for breakfast with a sprinkle of granola, enjoy it as a side with your lunch, or blend it into a refreshing smoothie for an afternoon snack.

In every town in Iceland, from bustling Reykjavik to the smallest coastal village, you'll find Skyr. It's available in supermarkets, local markets, and served in almost every café or restaurant. Look out for locally made Skyr, which often comes in a variety of flavors - from traditional plain to more adventurous options like blueberry or vanilla.

Finally, don't leave Iceland without trying Skyr cake. This tangy, creamy dessert is a crowd-pleaser, with its smooth Skyr filling and crunchy biscuit base. It's the perfect way to end a day of exploring, or to celebrate your new-found love for this traditional Icelandic product.

Lamb

The flavor of Icelandic lamb, tender and rich, reflects the country's pure, untamed nature. The sheep in Iceland spend their summers roaming freely, grazing on wild herbs and berries, which infuses the meat with a unique, delicate taste. You'll find that lamb is a key feature in many Icelandic meals, whether it's a succulent roast or a hearty stew.

Cooking styles vary across the country, but a common method is slow roasting, which allows the lamb's flavor to shine through. You might also come across smoked lamb, or hangikjöt, which is a traditional dish often served during Christmas but enjoyed year-round.

When it comes to finding the best places to try Icelandic lamb, seek out the local restaurants that source their meat directly from nearby farms. These establishments usually offer a variety of lamb dishes, so whether you prefer your lamb grilled, smoked, or slow-cooked, you're sure to find something that tickles your taste buds.

Fish and Seafood

Iceland's location in the North Atlantic means that the country has an abundant supply of fresh fish and seafood. From cod and haddock to shellfish like langoustines and mussels, Icelandic waters teem with a wide variety of seafood. Seafood dishes feature prominently in Icelandic cuisine, and you'll find that the freshness of the produce takes these dishes to another level.

A popular way to enjoy fish in Iceland is plokkfiskur, a comforting fish stew made with potatoes, onions, and a bechamel sauce. It's a simple dish, but incredibly satisfying, especially after a long day of sightseeing. If you're feeling adventurous, try the cured shark, or hákarl, which is a traditional Icelandic dish with a very distinct taste.

In terms of dining, you can't beat the seafood restaurants on the coast, where the catch of the day is often literally fresh off the boat. For a unique experience, head to one of the many fishing villages scattered around the country and dine in a local eatery. Here, you can enjoy the day's catch while overlooking the very waters the fish was caught in. It doesn't get fresher than that!

Rye Bread

Icelandic rye bread, or rúgbrauð, is a dense, dark bread that's traditionally baked in the ground using geothermal heat. This slow baking process gives the bread a unique, slightly sweet flavor that's unlike any other rye bread you might have tasted. It's the perfect accompaniment to a bowl of hearty Icelandic soup or a slab of smoked lamb.

Rúgbrauð is such a staple in Icelandic homes that you can find it in almost every grocery store or bakery. For a taste of tradition, you can visit places like the Laugarvatn Fontana, a geothermal bakery located in the Golden Circle area, where they still bake the bread in the ground.

When sampling rúgbrauð, remember to pair it with some Icelandic butter for an authentic experience. Or, for something a bit different, try it toasted with a slice of smoked trout on top. The mix of sweet, earthy bread and smoky, salty fish is a taste sensation not to be missed.

Hot Dogs

When it comes to street food in Iceland, the hot dog, or pylsa, is king. These aren't your average hot dogs, though. Made primarily from Icelandic lamb, along with a mix of pork and beef, Icelandic hot dogs have a unique flavor that's a world away from their American counterparts.

You'll find hot dog stands dotted all over Reykjavik and other towns, but for an iconic Icelandic experience, head to Bæjarins Beztu Pylsur in downtown Reykjavik. This humble hot dog stand has been serving up pylsur for over 80 years, and its fame has even attracted the likes of Bill Clinton and Kim Kardashian.

When ordering a hot dog in Iceland, the traditional way is "with everything." That means a topping of raw and fried onions, ketchup, sweet brown mustard called pylsusinnep, and a remoulade sauce. It's a combination of flavors that might sound unusual, but trust me, it works.

Traditional Fermented Shark

For the adventurous eaters out there, there's hákarl, or fermented shark. This traditional Icelandic dish is made from Greenland shark, a creature that's toxic to eat fresh due to high levels of ammonia. To make it safe to eat, the shark meat is fermented and then hung to dry for several months.

The result is a food that's famous for its strong smell and intense flavor. Eating hákarl has almost become a rite of passage for visitors to Iceland, with reactions ranging from delight to disgust. But don't let the descriptions deter you. You might end up loving it!

For a truly Icelandic experience, pair your hákarl with a shot of Brennivín, a local schnapps often referred to as "Black Death." You can find hákarl in most supermarkets and at traditional food markets. If you're in Reykjavik in late January, you might want to visit the Þorrablót festival, where hákarl is one of the traditional foods on offer.

Icelandic Candy

Icelandic candy is a unique world of flavors and textures that will keep your sweet tooth satisfied. Traditional Icelandic candies include liquorice, often paired with chocolate or marzipan; puffy, caramel-covered marshmallow treats known as "púffur"; and creamy toffees known as "móa".

One of the most iconic Icelandic candies is 'Opal', a small, lozenge-shaped candy that combines liquorice and menthol flavors. It's a rather acquired taste, but don't let that deter you from giving it a try. Head to any supermarket or candy store and get yourself an assortment of Icelandic sweets - it's a fun way to get a taste of the local culture.

While in Iceland, you might want to try some traditional candy-making techniques. In some parts of the country, candy is still made using geothermal heat, and visiting a geothermal candy factory can be a tasty and educational experience.

Local Dining Spots

Eating like a local is one of the best ways to truly immerse yourself in Icelandic culture. This could mean heading to a traditional bakery for some rúgbrauð, savoring a bowl of kæst skata (fermented skate) in someone's home on St. Thorlakur's Day, or tucking into a hearty lamb stew in a local tavern.

In Reykjavik, you'll find everything from Michelin-starred restaurants serving innovative Nordic cuisine, to family-run bistros dishing up hearty Icelandic classics. If you're traveling in the countryside, don't miss the chance to dine at a farm-to-table restaurant, where you can enjoy fresh local ingredients in a beautiful rural setting.

One thing's for sure, wherever you choose to dine, you'll find that Icelanders are passionate about their food and always happy to share it with visitors. So take the time to explore, taste, and discover the local cuisine - your taste buds will thank you.

Food Festivals

If you're a foodie, visiting Iceland during one of its food festivals can be a real treat. These events are a celebration of Icelandic cuisine and provide a unique opportunity to taste a wide variety of local dishes.

The Great Fish Day in Dalvík, held every August, is a must-visit event. It's a day when the whole town comes together to celebrate the local fishing industry, with stalls offering an endless variety of seafood dishes, all free of charge.

In February, the Reykjavík Winter Lights Festival brightens up the dark winter days with a host of cultural events, including a food and fun festival where top chefs showcase their culinary skills.

Whatever time of year you visit, keep an eye out for local food festivals and events. It's a great way to get to know the local food culture and try some delicious Icelandic dishes.

Regional Specialties

Each region in Iceland has its unique culinary specialties, shaped by local ingredients and traditions. In the Westfjords, for example, you'll find suðsuðeyri, a smoked lamb dish that's particularly popular during Christmas time. The Eastfjords are known for reindeer meat, which you can try in stews, steaks or as a topping on pizzas.

In the north, Akureyri, often referred to as the capital of North Iceland, is famed for its ice cream, regardless of the weather. Don't leave without trying a scoop or two. West Iceland, on the other hand, is famous for its dairy products, particularly its creamy and tangy skyr.

So, as you travel around the country, be sure to try the local specialties. Not only will you get a taste of the diverse Icelandic cuisine, but you'll also get a glimpse into the country's rich cultural tapestry.

Vegetarian and Vegan Cuisine

Despite the predominance of meat and fish in Icelandic cuisine, vegetarian and vegan options are becoming increasingly popular and accessible. From veggie dogs at Bæjarins Beztu Pylsur, Reykjavik's famous hot dog stand, to vegan ice-cream at Valdís, it's possible to enjoy plant-based versions of Icelandic classics.

Most restaurants in the larger cities now offer vegetarian and vegan options on their menus, and you can also find dedicated vegan restaurants. Glo, for instance, is a popular vegetarian restaurant in Reykjavik with a varied menu that will satisfy both vegetarians and vegans.

Even in the countryside, more and more places are offering plant-based dishes. It's always a good idea to ask about vegetarian and vegan options when dining out - you might be pleasantly surprised!

Final Thoughts

After reading through all these Icelandic culinary adventures, I hope your mouth is watering as much as mine is. Food is undeniably an integral part of any travel experience, and in Iceland, it's no different. The country's cuisine tells a tale of resilience, creativity, and a profound respect for the land and sea.

Whether you're savoring a bowl of hearty lamb stew, indulging in a bag of Icelandic candies, or feeling brave enough to try hákarl, the fermented shark, remember that every bite is a new experience, a new story.

At the end of the day, it's not just about the food itself, but the context in which it's enjoyed. It's the warmth of a bakery on a cold morning, the aroma of soup wafting from a kitchen in the middle of nowhere, the camaraderie in sharing a pot of skyr with new friends. These are the moments that make Icelandic cuisine so special.

So, buckle up, and prepare for an Icelandic culinary adventure. The Land of Fire and Ice is waiting, with a smorgasbord of flavors to discover. Skál!

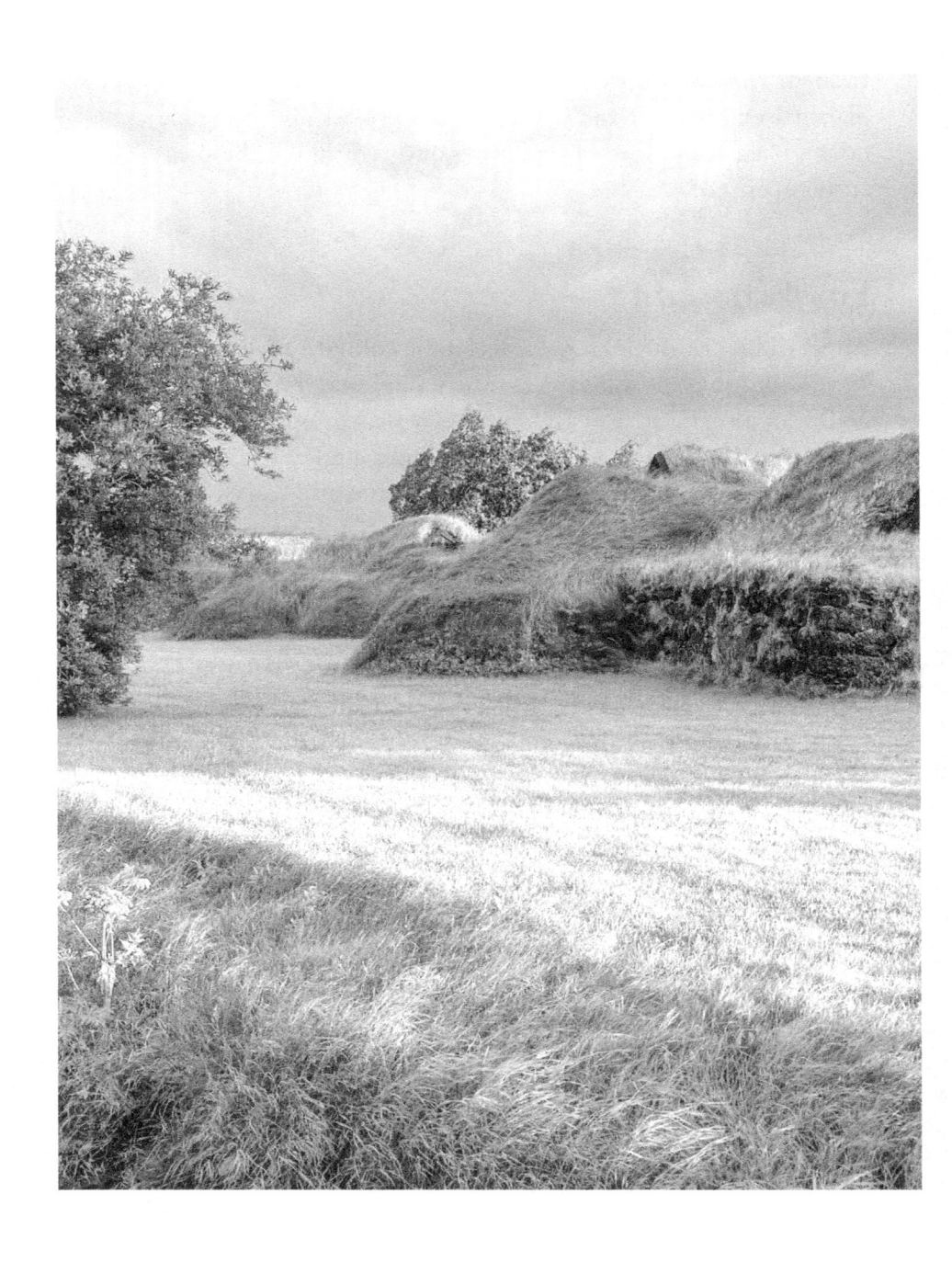

CHAPTER 11: HOW TO TRAVEL ON A BUDGET 153

CHAPTER 11:
How to Travel Iceland on a Budget

Ah, Iceland, the land of fire and ice, where ethereal landscapes meet raw natural power, a place where tiny fairies are believed to dwell amongst towering waterfalls and roaming sheep outnumber the human population. It's a destination that's on just about every traveler's bucket list, and with good reason. From the stunning beauty of the Northern Lights to the dramatic terrain that's like no other place on Earth, Iceland truly is a feast for the senses.

However, there's one thing that might be holding you back from booking that ticket: the cost. Iceland has a reputation for being one of the more expensive countries to visit. But don't let that deter you. Yes, while it's true that traveling in Iceland can be pricey, it doesn't mean it's impossible to explore this Nordic wonderland on a budget.

In this guide, we'll go through some tips and tricks that will help you make the most of your Icelandic adventure without breaking the bank. We'll talk about when to visit, where to stay, what to eat, how to get around, and much more. There will be no stone left unturned in our quest to provide you with the best advice for your budget journey.

Remember, travel isn't just about how much money you spend, but about the experiences you gather, the memories you make, and the stories you'll tell when you return. So, let's dive right in, shall we? Iceland's wonders await, even for the budget-conscious traveler.

Choosing the Right Time to Visit

Selecting the perfect time to visit Iceland can be a delicate balancing act. Of course, you want to see the country's stunning landscapes in all their glory. But you also need to keep an eye on your wallet. Most visitors flock to Iceland during the summer months, between June and August, when the weather is most pleasant and the daylight hours stretch into the night. However, this is also the peak season, meaning everything from airfares to accommodation rates will be at their highest.

That being said, visiting in the shoulder seasons (late April to May and September to October) can be a cost-effective alternative. Not only will you find cheaper rates for flights and accommodations, but also, the crowds will be thinner, making for a more peaceful exploration. Remember, Iceland's nature is stunning year-round, and each season brings its unique charm.

Also, if you're a fan of the Northern Lights, consider visiting between September and March. Not only are chances of seeing this natural wonder high, but you'll also find off-peak prices during these months. Just bear in mind that winter travel in Iceland can be challenging due to unpredictable weather and shorter daylight hours.

Accommodation

Accommodation is one of the biggest expenses when traveling, especially in a country like Iceland where the cost of living is high. Hotels in popular areas like Reykjavik or near major sights like the Golden Circle can set you back a fair bit. However, if you're open to alternatives, you can find ways to reduce this expense considerably.

Consider staying in guesthouses, hostels, or campsites. These options are not only cheaper but also offer a chance to meet fellow travelers and locals. If you're traveling in a group, renting a house or an apartment can be a cost-effective choice as you can split the cost. Remember, location is key. Staying a bit away from the city center or popular tourist spots can help you save. If you're up for an adventure, consider camping. Not only is it the cheapest form of accommodation, but waking up surrounded by Iceland's stunning nature is an experience money can't buy. Just make sure you are well-prepared for the weather and adhere to the country's camping regulations to ensure you leave no trace.

Food and Drinks

Food is another area where you can save money while traveling in Iceland. Eating out at restaurants, especially in touristy areas, can quickly add up. But that doesn't mean you have to miss out on trying Icelandic cuisine. You just need to be a bit savvy about it.

Visit local grocery stores and cook your own meals. This not only saves money but also allows you to explore Icelandic ingredients. Look out for discount supermarkets like Bónus or

Krónan where you can stock up on affordable food items. Also, remember that tap water in Iceland is pure and safe to drink, so refill your water bottle instead of buying bottled water.

If you still want to eat out occasionally, opt for lunch instead of dinner as many restaurants offer lunch specials at a reduced price. Or try the local hot dog stands, a favorite among Icelanders, that offer tasty and inexpensive meals. Also, don't forget to try the free samples at local markets. Just remember, it's all about balance – enjoy the local cuisine, but keep an eye on your budget.

Transportation

Getting around in Iceland is a significant part of the budget. Renting a car is a popular option among visitors as it provides the flexibility to explore at your own pace. However, rental rates, gas prices, and the potential need for a 4x4 vehicle can make this choice quite expensive. But fear not, there are some strategies to minimize these costs.

Firstly, consider sharing a rental car with other travelers. You can split the costs and share the driving. Also, book your car well in advance and shop around to find the best deal. And keep in mind that gas is cheaper in larger towns and cities than in rural areas, so plan your refueling accordingly.

Public transportation is another cost-effective way to get around. While it's not as flexible as driving, buses cover most major tourist sites, and in the summer, there are even bus passports covering various routes. Hitchhiking is also an option in Iceland, where it's generally safe and quite common, but always prioritize your safety.

Sightseeing and Attractions

When it comes to sightseeing, the good news is that many of Iceland's most stunning natural attractions are completely free to visit. From the waterfalls of Skógafoss and Seljalandsfoss to the geysers in the Golden Circle, you can feast your eyes on these wonders without spending a dime.

For attractions that do require an entry fee, look into combo tickets or tourist passes that can save you money if you're planning to visit multiple sites. Also, remember to take advantage of any discounts you might be eligible for, such as student or senior discounts. Consider guided tours carefully. While they can offer valuable insights and convenient transportation, they can also be pricey. Sometimes, exploring on your own or with a good guidebook can be just as fulfilling, and significantly cheaper. And if you're interested in museums, check for days when they offer discounted or free entry.

Shopping

Everyone likes to bring home a souvenir from their travels. However, shopping in Iceland can be expensive, given the high cost of living. But with a bit of strategy, you can still find affordable mementos of your trip.

Consider purchasing souvenirs from local markets rather than tourist-centric shops. These markets often feature handcrafted items from local artisans, which are not only unique but also support the local economy. Wool products, such as the iconic Icelandic sweater or "lopapeysa", are a popular choice.

Skip the duty-free stores at the airport and instead visit local supermarkets for cheap Icelandic goodies like chocolate or licorice. For book lovers, a novel by an Icelandic author could be a perfect souvenir. And remember, the best souvenirs are often free: take plenty of photos, collect small tokens from nature (without disturbing the environment), and most importantly, make unforgettable memories.

Avoiding Tourist Traps

Every travel destination has its fair share of tourist traps, and Iceland is no exception. While most places are genuinely worth your time and money, some might not offer the best value. Often, these are restaurants, shops, or attractions that are conveniently located but charge inflated prices.

Avoiding tourist traps mostly comes down to research. Read reviews of restaurants and attractions before you go. Often, places a bit further from the main tourist areas offer a more authentic experience at a better price. And don't be afraid to ask locals for recommendations - they'll know where to get the best value for your money.

Be wary of "free" tours. They can be a great way to explore, but remember that the guides usually work for tips, so they're not technically free. And while souvenir shops can be tempting, remember that the same items can often be found cheaper elsewhere. It's all about keeping your eyes open and making informed choices.

Using Local Currency

Iceland's currency is the Icelandic króna (ISK). While credit and debit cards are widely accepted, even in remote areas, having some cash on hand is still a good idea, especially for smaller purchases in places that may not accept cards, such as certain rural accommodations or markets.

ATMs are widely available and provide a convenient way to withdraw cash. However, be mindful of your bank's foreign transaction fees. Some travelers find it useful to bring a small amount of króna from their home country to avoid needing to find an ATM immediately upon arrival.

Keep an eye on the exchange rate, as it can fluctuate. And if a card machine gives you the option to pay in your home currency rather than króna, it's usually better to choose króna, as the conversion rate offered by card machines can be less favorable.

Travel Insurance

Travel insurance is a must-have for any trip, but it's particularly important when you're traveling on a budget. It can protect you from unforeseen costs due to travel disruptions, medical emergencies, or theft.

Many insurance policies cover trip cancellation or interruption, medical expenses, and lost or stolen belongings. Some also cover rental car damage, which could come in handy in Iceland's sometimes challenging driving conditions. Make sure you understand what's covered and what's not before you buy, and shop around to find the best rate.

In Iceland, emergency medical treatment is free or low-cost for European Health Insurance Card (EHIC) holders, but non-EU citizens will generally have to pay. It's worth noting that search and rescue operations in Iceland can be expensive, and if you're planning on hiking or exploring remote areas, there's specialized insurance for that. In the end, having travel insurance is all about peace of mind, allowing you to fully enjoy your trip without worry.

Bargaining

Iceland isn't really a country known for its haggling culture. Prices are usually set, whether you're shopping in a store, eating at a restaurant, or booking accommodation. It's not customary to bargain in these situations and trying to do so might be met with surprise or even disdain.

That being said, there might be some wiggle room if you're buying from a market stall or perhaps booking a long-term stay at a guesthouse, especially during the off-peak season. But even in these situations, be respectful and understand that the seller may not be open to negotiation.

If you're looking for a bargain, it's worth noting that the price of goods in Iceland is often reflective of the high cost of living and import costs. Shopping at budget-friendly stores, dining at cheaper local spots, planning your itinerary to include free or low-cost activities can help save money without needing to haggle.

Eco-friendly Practices

Iceland has a deep-rooted respect for nature, and preserving its stunning landscapes is a top priority. As a visitor, you can contribute to these efforts and make your trip more eco-friendly. Iceland has excellent recycling systems, so make use of them. Try to minimize single-use plastic by bringing a refillable water bottle – tap water in Iceland is some of the best in the world. Consider using public transportation or joining group tours instead of driving alone, to reduce carbon emissions. If you do rent a car, make sure to stick to marked roads and trails to avoid damaging fragile ecosystems.

Avoid touching or moving stones in mossy areas, as the moss is very delicate and takes decades to grow back. When visiting hot springs, make sure to shower without a swimsuit before entering, as requested, to keep the water clean for everyone. The aim should always be to leave no trace, preserving Iceland's beauty for future generations.

Final Thoughts

Traveling to Iceland on a budget might require some planning and a bit of a creative mindset, but it's absolutely doable. The stunning landscapes, vibrant culture, and warm-hearted locals make every penny spent worthwhile. Plus, there's a certain satisfaction that comes from finding ways to stretch your budget without sacrificing the quality of your experience.

When it comes to saving money in Iceland, remember that every little bit helps. A homemade picnic instead of a restaurant meal, a beautiful hike instead of a costly attraction, a shared ride instead of a private taxi – it all adds up. But the most important thing is to enjoy your journey, embrace the unexpected, and take home memories that will last a lifetime.

Finally, remember that while it's important to be conscious of your budget, it's also crucial to respect the environment and the local community. Being a responsible tourist not only helps preserve Iceland's natural beauty, but also makes the trip more rewarding for you. After all, the best things in Iceland – the stunning views, the midnight sun, the northern lights – are all free. So get out there, start exploring, and enjoy all the amazing experiences Iceland has to offer, even on a shoestring budget!

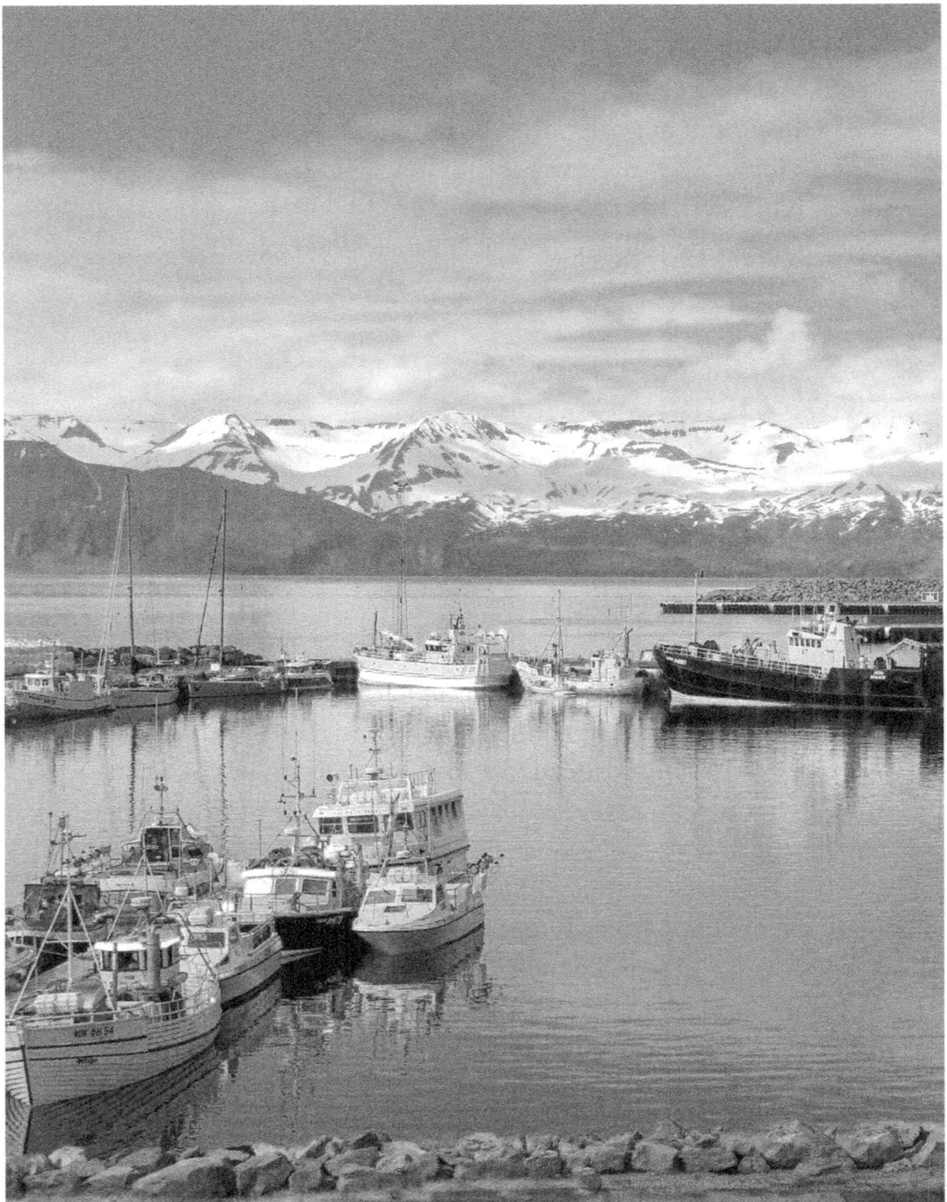

CHAPTER 12: 10 CULTURAL EXPERIENCES TO TRY 165

CHAPTER 12:
10 Cultural Experiences You Must Try in Iceland

There's no shortage of unique and captivating experiences to be had in the land of fire and ice. Iceland's cultural landscape is as diverse and dramatic as its natural one, filled with traditions that reach back to the ancient sagas, and fresh expressions of creativity that are carving out new paths. It's a place where folklore and innovation coexist, where nature's extremes inspire a way of life that's both resilient and full of joy.

From the moment you step foot in Iceland, you'll be welcomed into a world that encourages you to immerse yourself, to participate, to feel. Whether it's standing under the ethereal glow of the northern lights, savoring the comforting warmth of traditional Icelandic cuisine, or joining locals in a lively festival, there are experiences here that have the power to touch your heart and stir your soul.

What follows is a list of ten must-have cultural experiences in Iceland. They've been chosen for their ability to connect you to the heart of Icelandic culture, to provide a deeper understanding of this incredible place and its people. They're experiences that invite you to live as the Icelanders do, even if just for a while. This is not a checklist to rush through, but rather a set of opportunities to engage with the real Iceland, to let its spirit seep into you, to let it change you. Each experience is a doorway into a new aspect of Icelandic culture, and through these doorways, you can discover what makes Iceland so special.

So, if you're ready to venture beyond the surface, to step into a world where the extraordinary is just part of everyday life, here are ten cultural experiences you simply can't miss when visiting Iceland. Dive in, soak it up, and let the magic of Iceland work its wonders on you. Enjoy the journey!

1. Attending a Local Festival

Iceland has a rich tradition of festivals that span the entire calendar year, each bringing its unique flair and energy to the local scene. From the music-centric Iceland Airwaves, which turns Reykjavík into a city-wide venue for bands from around the world, to the quirky Þorrablót midwinter feast that features traditional Icelandic food like fermented shark, these celebrations offer an immersive peek into Icelandic culture.

A word of advice though: if you're planning to attend a local festival, book your accommodations early. These events are popular and can cause places to stay to fill up quickly. Also, don't hesitate to strike up a conversation with the locals. They're usually more than happy to share their customs and traditions with visitors.

2. Bathing in a Geothermal Pool

No trip to Iceland is complete without a dip in one of its many geothermal pools. It's a way of life for the locals, a daily routine as ingrained as a cup of morning coffee. From the Blue Lagoon's milky-blue waters to the countless local swimming pools found in every town, these naturally heated baths provide a soothing respite from Iceland's chilly climate.

When you visit, remember to shower before entering the pools – it's an Icelandic custom and shows respect for the local culture. Also, there's no need to worry if you forget your towel or swimsuit; most pools offer rental options. After your bath, join the locals in the poolside sauna or steam bath for the full experience.

3. Witnessing the Northern Lights

The aurora borealis, or the northern lights, is a natural spectacle like no other. Seeing these ethereal lights dance across the night sky is a mesmerizing experience that is simply unforgettable. While they can be elusive, your best chance to see them is during the colder months from late September to early April. Remember, patience is key when hunting for the northern lights. It might take several nights of waiting before you see them, and even then, there are no guarantees. Dress warmly, bring a thermos filled with hot chocolate or coffee, and embrace the adventure. Whether you're waiting under a star-filled sky in a remote countryside or witnessing the aurora from a thermal pool, it's an experience that's pure Iceland.

4. Visiting a Traditional Turf House

Icelandic turf houses, with their distinctive green roofs, are an iconic part of the country's cultural history. These houses were the primary form of housing in Iceland until the late 19th century and are a testament to the ingenuity of early Icelanders in adapting to their harsh environment. Locations such as the Skógasafn Open Air Museum or the historical farm at Keldur allow you to step back in time and experience what life was like in a turf house.

Don't just admire these houses from the outside; be sure to step in and experience the surprisingly cosy interiors. These houses were built to withstand the harsh Icelandic climate, and the thick turf provides excellent insulation. It's an incredible experience to sit in the same rooms where people lived centuries ago, protected from the elements by a layer of grass and soil.

Lastly, while these historical houses are robust, they're also delicate. Be respectful when you visit, follow all guidelines and instructions, and leave everything as you found it. These houses are a vital link to Iceland's past, and it's up to us to ensure they're around for future generations to appreciate.

5. Horse Riding

Horse riding is a deep-rooted tradition in Icelandic culture, tracing back to the Viking Age. The Icelandic horse is a unique breed known for its strength, endurance, and its special gait called the "tölt". Whether you're a seasoned rider or a complete beginner, exploring Iceland's vast lava fields, green valleys, and rugged mountain trails on horseback is a thrilling experience.

While riding, remember to respect the Icelandic horse's gentle nature. Listen to your guide's instructions and avoid startling the horse. Even if you're an experienced rider, take a moment to learn the "tölt". This smooth gait, unique to the Icelandic horse, provides a comfortable ride even over rough terrain.

Keep in mind that it's prohibited to import horses into Iceland, a law that protects the purity of the breed and prevents the introduction of diseases. As such, any horse that leaves the country can never return. This may seem harsh, but it's a testament to how deeply Icelanders care for these remarkable animals.

6. Whale Watching

Iceland is one of the best places in the world for whale watching, with over 20 different species frequenting its waters. From the playful white-beaked dolphins to the majestic humpback whales, the chance to see these magnificent creatures up close is a truly humbling experience. Towns like Husavik and Reykjavik offer regular whale-watching tours, most of which also include a knowledgeable guide.

Prepare for your whale-watching tour by dressing warmly, even in the summer. The temperature can drop considerably out on the open sea. Also, bring a pair of binoculars for a better view, and if you're prone to seasickness, don't forget your medication! Remember that patience is essential when it comes to whale watching. These creatures are wild and free, and sightings are never guaranteed. But that's part of the adventure! Even if you don't spot a whale, the breathtaking scenery and the chance to see other wildlife like puffins and seals make the journey worth it.

7. Hiking on a Glacier

Hiking on one of Iceland's monumental glaciers is an adventure like no other. Glaciers cover more than 10% of Iceland's land surface, and their ethereal blue ice and dramatic crevasses create a landscape that feels out of this world. Vatnajökull, Europe's largest glacier, and Sólheimajökull, a popular choice due to its accessibility, are two excellent locations for glacier hikes.

Safety should be your utmost priority while hiking on glaciers. It's crucial to hire an experienced guide and use the proper equipment. The ice can be slippery, and the glacier's surface can change rapidly due to weather conditions. Never venture onto a glacier without a guide or the necessary equipment; it's not just risky, but potentially lethal.

Lastly, while hiking, take a moment to appreciate the glacier's grandeur and beauty. Keep in mind, though, that these glaciers are receding rapidly due to climate change. Your visit is not just an adventure but a stark reminder of the importance of protecting our planet for future generations.

8. Experiencing Midnight Sun

The phenomenon of the midnight sun, where the sun remains visible at the local midnight, is something that must be experienced when visiting Iceland during summer. This natural event provides 24 hours of daylight, a magical experience that lends a surreal quality to the Icelandic landscapes. Whether you're capturing the glowing landscapes on your camera or simply basking in the ethereal light, the midnight sun is sure to be a highlight of your trip.

Take advantage of these extended daylight hours by planning late-night excursions. Imagine watching the sunset at midnight on a black sand beach or catching the reflection of the never-setting sun in a serene fjord. Just remember, it's easy to lose track of time under the midnight sun, so make sure you're still getting enough sleep!

Finally, while the midnight sun is a beautiful spectacle, it's also a reminder of Iceland's extreme geographical location. It's a phenomenon that you'll remember for years to come, offering a unique way to engage with the natural world that few places on Earth can match.

9. Sampling Traditional Icelandic Cuisine

The 9th must-have cultural experience in Iceland is sampling its traditional cuisine. Icelandic food is a direct reflection of the country's history and landscape, offering a unique blend of flavors. From the dairy-rich skyr to the fresh seafood and the hearty lamb dishes, Icelandic cuisine is sure to surprise and delight your palate.

When sampling traditional Icelandic cuisine, don't shy away from the more unusual dishes. Hakarl, fermented shark, might not be for the faint of heart, but it's a unique taste of Iceland's culinary history. Remember, part of the adventure of travel is trying new things, and that includes food!

Finally, don't forget to pair your meal with a glass of local beer or Brennivin, Iceland's signature schnapps. Icelanders are justifiably proud of their brewing and distilling traditions, and these beverages provide the perfect accompaniment to the country's hearty food. Enjoy your meal, and skál.

10. Experiencing a Traditional Icelandic Sagas Storytelling

Lastly, experiencing a traditional Icelandic Sagas storytelling is a must for cultural immersion. The Icelandic Sagas, written in the Old Norse language, are historical narratives that play a pivotal role in Iceland's literary tradition. They recount tales of the country's earliest settlers and their descendants, mixing historical facts with mythology and folklore.

The sagas are primarily centered around events that took place in the 10th and 11th centuries, during the age of settlement. While they recount tales of love, jealousy, and revenge, they also provide an extraordinary glimpse into the social structures, customs, and everyday life of the time.

Many places in Iceland offer saga storytelling sessions, where you can listen to these epic tales told in the traditional way, often around a cozy fire. Some sessions are even set in historical locations relevant to the sagas being recounted, enhancing the ambiance and bringing the stories to life. These narrative sessions offer an unforgettable connection to the country's history and culture, told in a truly captivating way.

Final Thoughts

Experiencing Iceland's unique culture is about more than just ticking items off a list; it's about immersing yourself in a fascinating country, engaging with its people, and connecting with its extraordinary landscapes. Each of these ten cultural experiences provides a different perspective on Iceland, showcasing the country's incredible diversity and its rich history.

Remember to approach each experience with an open mind and a spirit of adventure. You're not just observing a culture; you're actively participating in it. From the communal warmth of a geothermal pool to the breathtaking spectacle of the Northern Lights, each moment is an opportunity to engage more deeply with Iceland and its people.

And lastly, remember that every trip is personal. Your journey through Iceland might not include every item on this list, and that's perfectly okay. The most important thing is that you find the experiences that resonate most with you.

Iceland is a land of fire and ice, a place where the earth's raw power is on full display. It's also a country with a rich culture and a warm, welcoming people. So, whether you're hiking on a glacier, sampling traditional cuisine, or listening to the stirring narratives of ancient sagas, you're not just having an adventure – you're making memories that will last a lifetime. Safe travels, and enjoy your Icelandic journey!

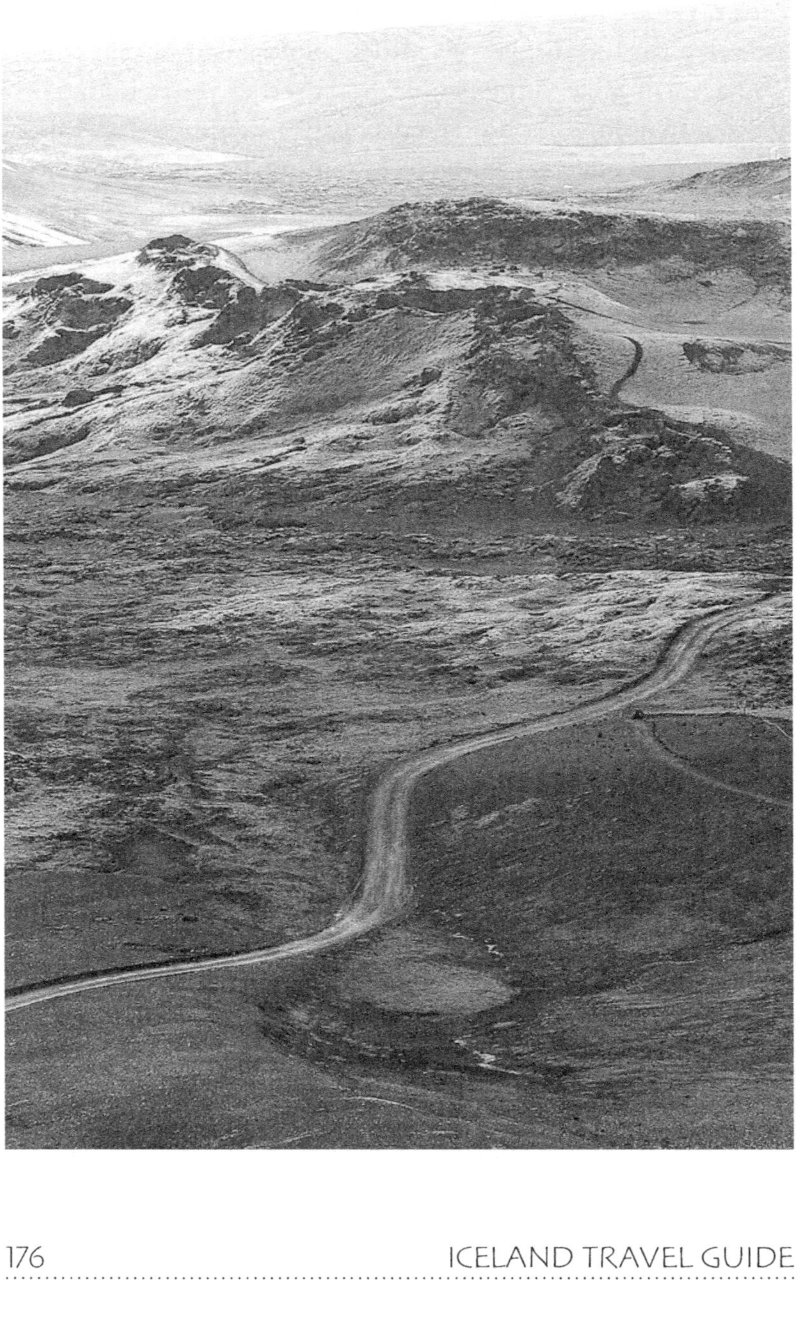

Conclusion

Iceland, the land of fire and ice, a place that defies easy description, where nature and culture intertwine in the most spectacular ways, has been our extraordinary journey's focus in this book. Unearthing its treasures chapter by chapter, we've painted a picture of a nation proud of its history, determinedly progressive, and welcoming to those who wish to partake in its splendor.

When you set foot in Iceland, you step into a realm where the earth is alive and active - geysers spurt skywards, waterfalls cascade into gaping chasms, and glaciers creak and crack as they flow slowly towards the sea. The power and the raw beauty of this land cannot be overstated. It is as inspiring as it is humbling, making every encounter with nature a moment of quiet introspection and unfiltered awe.

Yet, despite its wild heart, Iceland is a surprisingly accessible destination. It invites you to take part in its everyday rhythm, whether through its thriving food culture, the musical beat in Reykjavik's streets, or the hushed anticipation of Northern Lights hunters under a starlit sky. The nation has become a master at weaving its natural wonders into the fabric of everyday life.

This isn't a place where you simply 'go on holiday'; it's a land where you embark on a personal journey. Whether that journey involves marveling at the aurora borealis, soaking in a geothermal pool, or enjoying skyr under the midnight sun, the experience becomes part of you.

Travel in Iceland requires an open mind and a sense of adventure. The weather might be unpredictable, and the landscapes are often otherworldly, but it's this very unpredictability and distinctiveness that makes traveling here so unique. It is about letting go of rigid itineraries and embracing the unexpected. It's about stepping out of your comfort zone, whether that means trying fermented shark for the first time or getting lost in a saga's intricate narrative. Remember, though, that while adventures are at the heart of the Icelandic experience, it is equally crucial to respect the environment you explore. Stick to marked trails when hiking, don't venture onto glaciers without proper guidance, and remember the country's laws and regulations about off-road driving. It's about maintaining a balance - immersing yourself in Iceland's raw, untamed beauty while ensuring it remains that way for future generations.

As you prepare to embark on your Icelandic journey, it might be helpful to arm yourself with a few essential phrases in the local language. Not only does this show respect for the culture you're immersing yourself in, but it can also help break the ice and pave the way for memorable interactions. Here are some Icelandic phrases that could come in handy:

▷ "Halló" - Hello

▷ "Takk" - Thank you

▷ "Já" - Yes

▷ "Nei" - No

▷ "Hvar er klósett?" - Where is the toilet?

▷ "Hvað kostar þetta?" - How much is this?

- "Hvað heitir þú?" - What's your name?
- "Mig langar í kaffi" - I would like a coffee
- "Góðan dag" - Good day
- "Góða nótt" - Good night
- "Ég tala ekki íslensku" - I don't speak Icelandic
- "Hvar er næsta veitingahús?" - Where is the nearest restaurant?
- "Ég elska Ísland" - I love Iceland
- "Ég er týndur" - I'm lost
- "Getur þú hjálpað mér?" - Can you help me?

In the end, it's all about being open to new experiences, embracing different cultures, and being willing to go with the flow. And in a country as dynamic and vibrant as Iceland, the flow might take you to places you never imagined.

So here's to the journey, to the places you'll see and the people you'll meet along the way. Here's to the experiences that will challenge you, inspire you, and ultimately change you. Here's to Iceland, with all its fire and ice, its age-old sagas, and its warm-hearted people.

Remember, the beauty of travel lies not in the destination but in the journey itself. In the wise words of the great writer J.R.R. Tolkien, "Not all those who wander are lost." So go forth, wander, discover, and let Iceland's enchanting tapestry unfold before you. Skál (Cheers) to your Icelandic journey!

Final notes

You have reached the end of your journey through Iceland, probably one of the most appreciated destinations among travelers from all over the world. We hope that the suggested destinations and our advice will help you plan and enjoy your trip to the fullest.

The travel guide series of the Journey Joy collection was designed to be lean and straight to the point. The idea of keeping the guides short required significant work in synthesis, in order to guide the reader towards the essential destinations and activities within each country and city.

If you liked the book, leaving a positive review can help us spread our work. We realize that leaving a review can be a tedious activity, so we want to give you a gift. Send an email to **bonus@dedaloagency.net**, attach the screenshot of your review, and you will get completely **FREE**, in your mailbox, **THE UNRELEASED EBOOK**: "The Art of Traveling: Essential Tips for Unforgettable Journeys".

We thank you in advance and wish you to always travel and enjoy every adventure!

Made in the USA
Coppell, TX
14 June 2024